SIX
HOURS
ONE
FRIDAY

MAX LUCADO

SIX HOURS ONE FRIDAY

Anchoring to the Cross

MULTNOMAH

Portland, Oregon 97266

Unless otherwise indicated, all Scripture references are from the Holy Bible: New International Version, copyright 1973, 1978, 1984 by the International Bible Society. Used by permission of Zondervan Bible Publishers.

Scripture references marked Living Bible are from The Living Bible, copyright 1971 by Tyndale House Publishers, Wheaton, Ill. Used by permission.

Scripture references marked Jerusalem Bible are from The New Jerusalem Bible, copyright 1985 by Darton, Longman & Todd, Ltd., and Doubleday & Co., Inc.

Cover design by Bruce DeRoos

SIX HOURS, ONE FRIDAY
© 1989 by Max Lucado
Published by Multnomah Press
Portland, Oregon 97266

Multnomah Press is a ministry of Multnomah School of the Bible, 8435 N.E. Glisan Street, Portland, Oregon 97220

Printed in the United States

Library of Congress Cataloging-in-Publication Data

Lucado, Max.
    Six hours, one Friday : anchoring to the cross / Max Lucado.
      p. cm.
    ISBN 0-88070-314-8 hard
    ISBN 0-88070-376-8 paper
    1. Jesus Christ—Passion—Meditations.   I Title.
BT431.L795   1989
232.96—dc20   89-9429
                                                    CIP

   90 91 92 93 94 95 96 97 98 - 10 9 8 7 6 5 4 3

for
Jacquelyn, Joan, and Dee
from
your baby brother

This special Billy Graham Evangelistic Association edition is published with permission from the original publisher, Multnomah Press.

CONTENTS

ACKNOWLEDGEMENTS

This book was begun on one side of the equator and finished on the other. I've got people to thank in both places.

To the Christians in Rio de Janeiro, Brazil—Thanks for five thrilling years. Obrigado por tudo!

To the Christians at Oak Hills—Your faith and devotion are inspiring.

To Jim Toombs, Mike Cope, Rubel Shelley, Randy Mayeux, and Jim Woodroof—I appreciate the warm words and good advice.

To Ron Bailey—You gave the right counsel at the right time. Thanks.

To my relentless editor, Liz Heaney—I don't know how you do it, but you have a way of turning coal into diamonds.

To my secretary, Mary Stain—What would we do without you at the helm? Thanks for typing and typing and typing and. . .

To Marcelle LeGallo and Kathleen McCleery—Thank you for doing Mary's work so she could do mine.

And a special thanks to my wife Denalyn—You make coming home the highlight of my day.

CHAPTER 1

HURRICANE WARNINGS

Labor Day weekend, 1979. Throughout the nation people were enjoying their last waltz with summertime. Weekend reunions, camping trips, picnics.

Except in Miami.

While the rest of the nation played, the Gold Coast of south Florida watched. Hurricane David was whirling through the Caribbean, leaving a trail of flooded islands and homeless people.

Floridians don't have to be told to duck when a hurricane is on the warpath. Windows were taped up, canned goods were bought, flashlights were tested. David was about to pounce.

On the Miami River a group of single guys was trying to figure out the best way to protect their houseboat. Not that it was much of a vessel. It was, at best, a rustic cabin on a leaky barge. But it was home. And if they didn't do something, their home was going to be at the bottom of the river.

None of the fellows had ever lived on a boat before, much less weathered a hurricane. Any sailor worth his salt would have had a good laugh watching those landlubbers.

It was like a "McHale's Navy" rerun. They bought enough rope to tie up the *Queen Mary*. They had their boat tied to trees, tied to moorings, tied to herself. When they were through, the little craft looked as if she'd been caught in a spider's web. They were so busy tying her to everything, it's a wonder one of the guys didn't get tied up.

How was I privy to such a fiasco? You guessed it. The houseboat was mine.

Don't ask what I was doing with a houseboat. Part adventure and part bargain, I guess. But that Labor Day weekend was more adventure than I'd bargained for. I had owned the boat for three monthly payments and now I was about to have to sacrifice her to the hurricane! I was desperate. *Tie her down!* was all I could think.

I was reaching the end of my rope, in more ways than one, when Phil showed up. Now Phil knew boats. He even looked boat-wise.

He was born wearing a suntan and dock-siders. He spoke the lingo and knew the knots. He also knew hurricanes. Word on the river had it that he had ridden one out for three days in a ten-foot sailboat. They made him a living legend.

He felt sorry for us, so he came to give some advice . . . and it was sailor-sound. "Tie her to land

and you'll regret it. Those trees are gonna get eaten by the 'cane. Your only hope is to anchor deep," he said. "Place four anchors in four different locations, leave the rope slack, and pray for the best."

Anchor deep. Good advice. We took it and . . . well, before I tell you whether or not we handled the hurricane, let's talk about anchor points.

Chances are someone reading these words is about to get caught in a storm. The weather is brewing and the water is rising and you can see the trees beginning to bend.

> You've done everything possible but your marriage still won't stand. It's just a matter of time.

> You bit off more than you could chew. You never should have agreed to take on an assignment like that. There is no way you can meet the deadline. And when that due date comes and you don't produce. . . .

> You've been dreading this meeting all week. They've already laid off several men. Why else would the personnel director need to talk to you? And with a newborn at home.

Perhaps the winds have already reached gale force and you're holding on for your life.

> "Why our son?" are the only words you can muster. The funeral is over and the words of comfort have been politely said. Now it is just you, your memories, and your question, "Why me?"

"The tests were positive. The tumor is malignant." Just when you thought the biggest struggle was over. More surgery.

"They took the other bid." That sale was your last hope. To be outbid could mean you'll have to shut down the shop. That client would have been just enough to keep the business afloat for another quarter. But now?

Waves that suck our joy out to sea. Winds that rip out our hopes by their roots. Rising tides that seep under the doors of our lives and cover the floors of our hearts.

I got caught in a hurricane as this chapter was being completed. The warning came in a telephone call during a meeting. The forecaster with the grim news was my wife. "Max, your sister just called. Your mother is going to have quadruple bypass surgery at eight o'clock tomorrow morning." A few quick calls to the airlines. Clothes thrown in a bag. A race to the airport in time to grab the last seat on the last flight.

No time to develop a personal philosophy on pain and suffering. No time to analyze the mystery of death. No time to set anchors. Time only to sit tight and trust the anchor points.

Anchor points. Firm rocks sunk deeply in a solid foundation. Not casual opinions or negotiable hypotheses, but ironclad undeniables that will keep you afloat. How strong are yours? How sturdy is your life when faced with one of these three storms?

Futility. You're riding high and getting higher. You should be content. You should be pleased. You are doing what you set out to do. You have a house.

You have a job. You have security. You have two cars in the garage and a CD in the bank. By everyone's estimations you should be pleased.

Then why are you so unhappy? Is it because you know that every tide that rises also falls? Is it because your degree and promotion don't answer the questions that keep you awake at night? "What's it for, anyway?" "Who will know what I did?" "Who cares who I am?" "What is the purpose of it all?"

Failure. You can't hide it anymore. You blew it. You were wrong. You let everyone down. Instead of standing tall, you fell short. Instead of stepping out, you stepped back. The very thing you swore you'd never do is exactly what you did.

Your anchors drag through sand, finding no rocks. Unless a solid point is found soon, the hull of your heart will be splintered.

Finality. The scene repeats itself thousands of times each day in America. Folding chairs on manicured grass. Nicely dressed people under a canvas canopy. Kleenexes. Tears. Words. Metal casket. Flowers. Dirt. Open grave.

It's the wave of finality.

Though it has slapped the beach countless times, you never considered it would hit you, but it did. Uninvited and unexpected, it hit with tidal force, washing away your youth, your innocence, your mate, your friend. And now you're soaked and shivering, wondering if you will be next.

Futility,
        failure,
                finality.

You don't have to face these monsters alone. Listen to Phil's advice. It's sailor-sound both in and out of the water: Anchor deep.

Got any hurricanes coming your way?

This book examines three anchor points. Three boulders which can stand against any storm. Three rocks that repel the tallest of waves. Three petrified ledges to which you can hook your anchors. Each anchor point was planted firmly in bedrock two thousand years ago by a carpenter who claimed to be the Christ. And it was all done in the course of a single day. A single Friday. All done during six hours, one Friday.

To the casual observer there was nothing unusual about these six hours. To the casual observer, this Friday was a normal Friday. Six hours of routine. Six hours of the expected.

Six hours. One Friday.

Enough time for:

> a shepherd to examine his flocks.
> a housewife to clean and organize her house.
> a physician to receive a baby from a mother's womb and cool the fever of one near death.

Six hours. From 9:00 A.M. to 3:00 P.M.

Six hours. One Friday.

Six hours filled with, as are all hours, the mystery of life.

The bright noonday sun casts a common shadow for the Judean countryside. It's the black silhouette of a shepherd standing near his fat-tailed flock. He stares at the clear sky, searching for clouds. There are none.

He looks back at his sheep. They graze lazily on the rocky hillside. An occasional sycamore provides shade. He sits on the slope and places a blade of grass in his mouth. He looks beyond the flock at the road below.

For the first time in days, the traffic is thin. For over a week a river of pilgrims has streamed through this valley, bustling down the road with animals and loaded carts. For days he has watched them from his perch. Though he couldn't hear them, he knew they were speaking a dozen different dialects. And though he didn't talk to them, he knew where they were going and why.

They were going to Jerusalem. And they were going to sacrifice lambs in the temple.

The celebration strikes him as ironic. Streets jammed with people. Marketplaces full of the sounds of the bleating of goats and the selling of birds.

Endless observances.

The people relish the festivities. They awaken early and retire late. They find strange fulfillment in the pageantry.

Not him.

What kind of God would be appeased by the death of an animal?

Oh, the shepherd's doubts are never voiced anywhere except on the hillside. But on this day, they shout.

It isn't slaughter of the animals that disturbs him. It is the endlessness of it all. How many years has he seen the people come and go? How many caravans? How many sacrifices? How many bloody carcasses?

Memories stalk him. Memories of uncontrolled anger . . . uncontrolled desire . . . uncontrolled anxiety. So many mistakes. So many stumbles. So much guilt. God seems so far away. *Lamb after lamb. Passover after Passover. Yet I still feel the same.*

He turns his head and looks again at the sky. Will the blood of yet another lamb really matter?

The wife sits in her house. It's Friday. She's alone. Her husband, a priest, is at the temple. It's time for lunch, but she has no appetite. Besides, it's hardly worth the trouble to prepare a meal for one. So, she sits and looks out the window.

The narrow street in front of her house is thick with people. Were she younger, she would be out there. Even if she had no reason to go on the streets, she would go. There was a time when she was energized by such activity. Not now. Now her hair is gray. Her face is wrinkled, and she is tired.

For years she has observed the holidays. For years she has watched the people. Many summers have passed, taking with them her youth and leaving only the perplexities that hound her.

As a young woman she was too busy to ponder. She had children to raise. Meals to prepare. Schedules to keep. She brushed away the riddles like she brushed back her hair. But now her home was empty. Those who needed her have others who need them. Now, the questions are relentless. Who am I? Where did I come from? Where am I going? Why is it all happening?

The house is alive with excitement. In one room a man paces. In another a woman pushes. Sweat-beads glisten on her forehead. Her eyes close, then open. She laughs, then groans. The young doctor encourages her. "Not much more. Don't give up." With a deep breath she leans forward and exerts her last ounce of energy. Then she leans back, pale and spent.

"You have a son." She raises her head just enough to see the red infant cradled in the broad palms of the physician.

Delighted with his task, the doctor cleans the eyes and smiles as he watches them fight to open. The child, freshly welcomed from the womb, is returned to his mother.

The next house he visits is quiet. Outside the bedroom a white-haired wife sits. Inside is the frail frame of her husband, hot with fever. Nothing can be done. The doctor is helpless as the man takes his last breath. It's deep—his bony, bare chest rises. His mouth opens wide, so wide that his lips whiten. Then he dies.

The same hands that cleansed the eyes of the infant now close the eyes of the dead. All during a period of six hours on one Friday.

He fights off the questions. He hasn't time to hear them today. But they are stubborn and demand to be heard.

Why heal the sick only to postpone death?

Why give strength only to see it ebb away?

Why be born and then begin to die?

Who points the crooked finger at death's next victim?

Who is this one that with such regular randomness separates soul from body?

He shrugs and places the sheet over the ashening face.

Six hours, one Friday.

To the casual observer the six hours are mundane. A shepherd with his sheep, a housewife with her thoughts, a doctor with his patients. But to the handful of awestruck witnesses the most maddening of miracles is occurring.

God is on a cross. The creator of the universe is being executed.

Spit and blood are caked to his cheeks and his lips are cracked and swollen. Thorns rip his scalp. His lungs scream with pain. His legs knot with cramps. Taut nerves threaten to snap as pain twangs her morbid melody. Yet, death is not ready. And there is no one to save him, for he is sacrificing himself.

It is no normal six hours . . . it is no normal Friday.

Far worse than the breaking of his body is the shredding of his heart.

His own countrymen clamored for his death.

His own disciple planted the kiss of betrayal.

His own friends ran for cover.

And now his own father is beginning to turn his back on him, leaving him alone.

A witness could not help but ask: Jesus, do you give no thought to saving yourself? What keeps you there? What holds you to the cross? Nails don't hold gods to trees. What makes you stay?

The shepherd stands staring at the now blackened sky. Only seconds before he had stared at the sun. Now there is no sun.

The air is cool. The sky is black. No thunder. No lightening. No clouds. The sheep are restless. The feeling is eerie. The shepherd stands alone, wondering and listening.

What is this hellish darkness? What is this mysterious eclipse? What has happened to the light?

There is a scream in the distance. The shepherd turns toward Jerusalem.

A soldier, unaware that his impulse is part of a divine plan, plunges the spear into the side. The blood of the Lamb of God comes forth and cleanses.

The woman has scarcely lit the lamp when her husband rushes in the door. The reflection of the lamp's flame dances wildly in his wide eyes. "The temple curtain . . .," he begins breathlessly, "Torn! Ripped in two from top to bottom!"

The black angel hovers over the one on the center cross.

No delegation for this death, no demon for this duty. Satan has reserved this task for himself. Gleefully, he passes his hand of death over these eyes of life.

But just when the last breath escapes, the war begins.

The pit of the earth rumbles. The young physician nearly loses his balance.

It is an earthquake—a rock-splitting rumble. A stampede-like vibration, as if prison doors have been opened and the captives are thundering to freedom. The doctor fights to keep his balance as he hurries back to the room of the one who has just died.

The body is gone.

Six hours. One Friday.

Let me ask you a question: What do you do with that day in history? What do you do with its claims?

If it really happened . . . if God did commandeer his own crucifixion . . . if he did turn his back on his own son . . . if he did storm Satan's gate, then those six hours that Friday were packed with tragic triumph. If that was God on that cross, then the hill called Skull is a granite studded with stakes to which you can anchor.

Those six hours were no normal six hours. They were the most critical hours in history. For during those six hours on that Friday, God embedded in the earth three anchor points sturdy enough to withstand any hurricane.

Anchor point #1—*My life is not futile.* This rock secures the hull of your heart. Its sole function is to give you something which you can grip when facing the surging tides of futility and relativism. It's a firm grasp on the conviction that there is truth. Someone is in control and I have a purpose.

Anchor point #2—*My failures are not fatal.* It's not that he loves what you did, but he loves who you are. You are his. The one who has the right to condemn you provided the way to acquit you. You make mistakes. God doesn't. And he made you.

Anchor point #3—*My death is not final.* There is one more stone to which you should tie. It's large. It's round. And it's heavy. It blocked the door of a grave. It wasn't big enough, though. The tomb that it sealed was the tomb of a transient. He only went in to prove he could come out. And on the way out he took the stone with him and turned it into an anchor point. He dropped it deep into the uncharted waters of death. Tie to his rock and the typhoon of the tomb becomes a spring breeze on Easter Sunday.

There they are. Three anchor points. The anchor points of the cross.

Oh, by the way, Hurricane David never made it to Miami. Thirty minutes off the coast he decided to bear north. The worst damage my boat suffered were some rope burns inflicted by her overzealous crew.

I hope your hurricane misses you, too. But in case it doesn't, take the sailor's advice. "Anchor deep, say a prayer, and hold on.'' And don't be surprised if someone walks across the water to give you a hand.

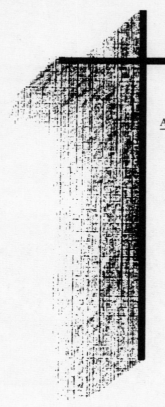

MY LIFE
IS NOT
FUTILE

CHAPTER 2

GOD'S FORMULA FOR FATIGUE

It's late. It's past the bed-time hour. They think I'm studying. They think I think they're going to sleep. I know better. Too many giggles. Too many whispers. Too many trips to the closet to get another doll. Too many dashes in the dark to trade pillows.

It's late. It's time for little girls to be going to sleep. But for four-year-old Jenna and two-year-old Andrea, sleep is the last item on their list of things to do.

Here's the list.

Andrea still needs to flip on her back and let her feet hang out the crib a bit.

Jenna will fluff her pillow, then fluff her pillow and, well, it still needs a little fluffing.

Andrea will scoot from one side of the bed to the other.

Jenna has yet to count her fingers in a whisper and pump her make-believe bicycle.

And before sleep settles over them, more juice will be requested, another song will be sung, and a story will be told.

I love it. It's a game. The contestants? Childhood joy and sleepy eyes. The name of the game? Catch-me-if-you-can.

Sleep is determined to bring the day to a close and joy is determined to stretch the day out as long as possible. One last enchanted kingdom. One last giggle. One last game.

Maybe you are like that. Maybe, if you had your way, your day would never end. Every moment demands to be savored. You resist sleep as long as possible because you love being awake so much. If you are like that, congratulations. If not, welcome to the majority.

Most of us have learned another way of going to bed, haven't we? It's called crash and burn. Life is so full of games that the last thing we want is another one as we are trying to sleep. So, for most of us, it's good-bye world, hello pillow. Sleep, for many, is not a robber but a refuge; eight hours of relief for our wounded souls.

And if you are kept awake, it's not by counting your fingers, but by counting your debts, tasks, or even your tears.

You are tired.

You are weary.

Weary of being slapped by the waves of broken dreams.

Weary of being stepped on and run over in the endless marathon to the top.

Weary of trusting in someone only to have that trust returned in an envelope with no return address.

Weary of staring into the future and seeing only futility.

What steals our childhood zeal? For a child, the possibilities are limitless.

Then weariness finds us. Sesame Street gets traffic-jammed. Dreams of Peter Pan are buried with Grandpa. And Star Trek's endless horizon gets hidden behind smog and skyscrapers.

What is the source of such weariness? What are the names of these burdens?

In this book we are looking at three. Futility, failure, and finality. The three Fs on the human report card. The three burdens that are too big for any back, too heavy for any biceps. Three burdens that no man can carry alone.

Let's look at futility. Few things can weary you more than the fast pace of the human race. Too many sprints for success. Too many laps in the gray-flannel fast-lane. Too many nine-to-five masquerade parties. Too many days of doing whatever it takes, eventually take their toll. You are left gasping for air, holding your sides on the side of the track.

And it isn't the late night reports or countless airports that sap your strength as much as it is the question you dare not admit that you are asking yourself. *Is it worth it? When I get what I want, will it be worth the price I paid?*

Perhaps those were the thoughts of a San Antonio lawyer I read about recently. Successful, well-paid, new wife, remodeled house. But apparently it wasn't enough. One day, he came home, took a gun out of his vault, climbed into a sleeping bag, and took his life. His note to his bride read, "It's not that I don't love you. It's just that I'm tired and I want to rest."

It is this weariness that makes the words of the carpenter so compelling. Listen to them. "Come to me, all you who are weary and burdened and I will give you rest."[1]

Come to me. . . . The invitation is to come to him. Why him?

He offers the invitation as a penniless rabbi in an oppressed nation. He has no political office, no connections with the authorities in Rome. He hasn't written a best-seller or earned a diploma.

Yet, he dares to look into the leathery faces of farmers and tired faces of housewives and offer rest. He looks into the disillusioned eyes of a preacher or two from Jerusalem. He gazes into the cynical stare of a banker and the hungry eyes of a bartender and makes this paradoxical promise: "Take my yoke upon you and learn from me, for I am gentle and humble in heart, and you will find rest for your souls."[2]

The people came. They came out of the cul-de-sacs and office complexes of their day. They brought him the burdens of their existence and he gave them, not religion, not doctrine, not systems, but rest.

As a result, they called him Lord.

As a result, they called him Savior.

Not so much because of what he said, but because of what he did.

What he did on the cross during six hours, one Friday.

On the following pages you will see several people. They may be new to you, or they may be old acquaintances. They have one thing in common—they came to Jesus weary with the futility of life. A rejected woman. A confused patriarch. Disoriented disciples. A discouraged missionary.

They all found rest. They found anchor points for their storm-tossed souls. And they found that Jesus was the only man to walk God's earth who claimed to have an answer for man's burdens. "Come to me," he invited them.

My prayer is that you, too, will find rest. And that you will sleep like a baby.

1. Matthew 11:28   2. Matthew 11:29

CHAPTER 3

TWO TOMBSTONES

I had driven by the place countless times. Daily I passed the small plot of land on the way to my office. Daily I told myself, "Someday I need to stop there."

Today, that "someday" came. I convinced a tight-fisted schedule to give me thirty minutes and I drove in.

The intersection appears no different from any other in San Antonio: a Burger King, a Rodeway Inn, a restaurant. But turn northwest, go under the cast-iron sign, and you will find yourself on an island of history that is holding its own against the river of progress.

The name on the sign? Locke Hill Cemetery.

As I parked, a darkened sky threatened rain. A lonely path invited me to walk through the two-hundred-plus tombstones. The fatherly oak trees arched above me, providing a ceiling for the solemn chambers. Tall grass, still wet from the morning dew, brushed my ankles.

The tombstones, though weathered and chipped, were alive with yesterday.

Ruhet in herrn accents the markers that bear names like Schmidt, Faustman, Grundmeyer, and Eckert.

Ruth Lacey is buried there. Born in the days of Napoleon—1807. Died over a century ago—1877.

I stood on the same spot where a mother wept on a cold day some eight decades past. The tombstone read simply, "Baby Boldt—Born and died December 10, 1910."

Eighteen-year-old Harry Ferguson was laid to rest in 1883 under these words, "Sleep sweetly tired young pilgrim." I wondered what wearied him so.

Then I saw it. It was chiseled into a tombstone on the northern end of the cemetery. The stone marks the destination of the body of Grace Llewellen Smith. No date of birth is listed, no date of death. Just the names of her two husbands, and this epitaph:

> "Sleeps, but rests not.
> Loved, but was loved not.
> Tried to please, but pleased not.
> Died as she lived—alone."

Words of futility.

I stared at the marker and wondered about Grace Llewellen Smith. I wondered about her life. I wondered if she'd written the words . . . or just lived them. I wondered if she deserved the pain. I wondered if she was bitter or beaten. I wondered if she was plain. I wondered if she was beautiful. I wondered why some lives are so fruitful while others are so futile.

I caught myself wondering aloud, "Mrs. Smith, what broke your heart?"

Raindrops smudged my ink as I copied the words.

Loved, but was loved not . . .

Long nights. Empty beds. Silence. No response to messages left. No return to letters written. No love exchanged for love given.

Tried to please, but pleased not . . .

I could hear the hatchet of disappointment.

"How many times do I have to tell you?" Chop.

"You'll never amount to anything." Chop. Chop.

"Why can't you do anything right?" Chop, chop, chop.

Died as she lived—alone.

How many Grace Llewellen Smiths are there? How many people will die in the loneliness in which they are living? The homeless in Atlanta. The happy-hour hopper in L.A. A bag lady in Miami. The preacher in Nashville. Any person who doubts whether the world needs him. Any person who is convinced that no one really cares.

Any person who had been given a ring, but never a heart; criticism, but never a chance; a bed, but never rest.

These are the victims of futility.

And unless someone intervenes, unless something happens, the epitaph of Grace Smith will be theirs.

That's why the story you are about to read is significant. It's the story of another tombstone. This time, however, the tombstone doesn't mark the death of a person—it marks the birth.[1]

Her eyes squint against the noonday sun. Her shoulders stoop under the weight of the water jar. Her feet trudge, stirring dust on the path. She keeps her eyes down, so she can dodge the stares of the others.

She is a Samaritan; she knows the sting of racism. She is a woman; she's bumped her head on the ceiling of sexism. She's been married to five men. Five. Five different marriages. Five different beds. Five different rejections. She knows the sound of slamming doors.

She knows what it means to love and receive no love in return. Her current mate won't even give her his name. He only gives her a place to sleep.

If there is a Grace Llewellen Smith in the New Testament, it is this woman. The epitaph of insignificance could have been hers. And it would have been except for an encounter with a stranger.

On this particular day, she came to the well at noon. Why hadn't she gone in the early morning with the other women? Maybe she had. Maybe she just needed an extra draw of water on a hot day. Or maybe not. Maybe it was the other women she was avoiding. A walk in the hot sun was a small price to pay in order to escape their sharp tongues.

"Here she comes."

"Have you heard? She's got a new man!"

"They say she'll sleep with anyone."

"Shhh. There she is."

So she came to the well at noon. She expected silence. She expected solitude. Instead, she found one who knew her better than she knew herself.

He was seated on the ground: legs outstretched, hands folded, back resting against the well. His eyes were closed. She stopped and looked at him. She looked around. No one was near. She looked back at him. He was obviously Jewish. What was he doing here? His eyes opened and hers ducked in embarrassment. She went quickly about her task.

Sensing her discomfort, Jesus asked her for water. But she was too streetwise to think that all he wanted was a drink. "Since when does an uptown fellow like you ask a girl like me for water?" She wanted to know what he really had in mind. Her intuition was partly correct. He was interested in more than water. He was interested in her heart.

They talked. Who could remember the last time a man had spoken to her with respect?

He told her about a spring of water that would quench, not the thirst of the throat, but of the soul.

That intrigued her. "Sir, give me this water so that I won't get thirsty and have to keep coming here to draw water."

"Go, call your husband and come back."

Her heart must have sunk. Here was a Jew who didn't care if she was a Samaritan. Here was a man who didn't look down on her as a woman. Here was the closest thing to gentleness she'd ever seen. And now he was asking her about . . . that.

Anything but that. Maybe she considered lying. "Oh, my husband? He's busy." Maybe she wanted to change the subject. Perhaps she wanted to leave—but she stayed. And she told the truth.

"I have no husband." (Kindness has a way of inviting honesty.)

You probably know the rest of the story. I wish you didn't. I wish you were hearing it for the first time. For if you were, you'd be wide-eyed as you waited to see what Jesus would do next. Why? Because you've wanted to do the same thing.

You've wanted to take off your mask. You've wanted to stop pretending. You've wondered what God would do if you opened your cobweb-covered door of secret sin.

This woman wondered what Jesus would do. She must have wondered if the kindness would cease when the truth was revealed. *He will be angry. He will leave. He will think I'm worthless.*

If you've had the same anxieties, then get out your pencil. You'll want to underline Jesus' answer.

"You're right. You have had five husbands and the man you are with now won't even give you a name."

No criticism? No anger? No what-kind-of-mess-have-you-made-of-your-life lectures?

No. It wasn't perfection that Jesus was seeking, it was honesty.

The woman was amazed.

"I can see that you are a prophet." Translation? "There is something different about you. Do you mind if I ask you something?"

Then she asked the question that revealed the gaping hole in her soul.

"Where is God? My people say he is on the mountain. Your people say he is in Jerusalem. I don't know where he is."

I'd give a thousand sunsets to see the expression on Jesus' face as he heard those words. Did his eyes water? Did he smile? Did he look up into the clouds and wink at his father? Of all the places to find a hungry heart—Samaria?

Of all the Samaritans to be searching for God— a woman?

Of all the women to have an insatiable appetite for God—a five-time divorcée?

And of all the people to be chosen to personally receive the secret of the ages—an outcast among outcasts? The most "insignificant" person in the region?

Remarkable. Jesus didn't reveal the secret to King Herod. He didn't request an audience of the Sanhedrin and tell them the news. It wasn't within the colonnades of a Roman court that he announced his identity.

No, it was in the shade of a well in a rejected land to an ostracized woman. His eyes must have danced as he whispered the secret.

"I am the Messiah."

The most important phrase in the chapter is one easily overlooked. "Then, leaving her water jar, the woman went back to the town and said to the people, 'Come, see a man who told me everything I ever did. Could this be the Christ?' "[2]

Don't miss the drama of the moment. Look at her eyes, wide with amazement. Listen to her as she struggles for words. "Y-y-y-you a-a-a-are the M-m-m-messiah!" And watch as she scrambles to her feet, takes one last look at this grinning Nazarene, turns and runs right into the burly chest of Peter. She almost falls, regains her balance, and hotfoots it toward her home town.

Did you notice what she forgot? She forgot her water jar. She left behind the jug that had caused the sag in her shoulders. She left behind the burden she brought.

Suddenly the shame of the tattered romances disappeared. Suddenly the insignificance of her life was swallowed by the significance of the moment. "God is here! God has come! God cares . . . for me!"

That is why she forgot her water jar. That is why she ran to the city. That is why she grabbed the first person she saw and announced her discovery, "I just talked to a man who knows everything I ever did . . . and he loves me anyway!"

The disciples offered Jesus some food. He refused it—he was too excited! He had just done what he does best. He had taken a life that was drifting and given it direction.

He was exuberant!

"Look!" he announced to disciples, pointing at the woman who was running to the village. "Vast fields of human souls are ripening all around us, and are ready now for the reaping."[3]

Who could eat at a time like this?

For some of you the story of these two women is touching but distant. You belong. You are needed and you know it. You've got more friends than you can visit and more tasks than you can accomplish.

Insignificance will not be chiseled on your tombstone.

Be thankful.

But others of you are different. You paused at the epitaph because it was yours. You see the face of Grace Smith when you look into the mirror. You know why the Samaritan woman was avoiding people. You do the same thing.

You know what it's like to have no one sit by you at the cafeteria. You've wondered what it would be like to have one good friend. You've been in love and you wonder if it is worth the pain to do it again.

And you, too, have wondered where in the world God is.

I have a friend named Joy who teaches under-privileged children in an inner city church. Her class is a lively group of nine-year-olds who love life and aren't afraid of God. There is one exception, however—a timid girl by the name of Barbara.

Her difficult home life had left her afraid and insecure. For the weeks that my friend was teaching the class, Barbara never spoke. Never. While the other children talked, she sat. While the others sang, she was silent. While the others giggled, she was quiet.

Always present. Always listening. Always speechless.

Until the day Joy gave a class on heaven. Joy talked about seeing God. She talked about tearless eyes and deathless lives.

Barbara was fascinated. She wouldn't release Joy from her stare.

She listened with hunger. Then she raised her hand. "Mrs. Joy?"

Joy was stunned. Barbara had never asked a question. "Yes, Barbara?"

"Is heaven for girls like me?"

Again, I would give a thousand sunsets to have seen Jesus' face as this tiny prayer reached his throne. For indeed that is what it was—a prayer.

An earnest prayer that a good God in heaven would remember a forgotten soul on earth. A prayer that God's grace would seep into the cracks and cover one the church let slip through. A prayer to take a life that no one else can use and use it as no one else can.

Not a prayer from a pulpit; but one from a bed in a convalescent home. Not a prayer prayed confidently by black-robed seminarian; but one whispered fearfully by a recovering alcoholic.

A prayer to do what God does best: take the common and make it spectacular. To once again take the rod and divide the sea. To take a pebble and kill a Goliath. To take water and make sparkling wine. To take a peasant boy's lunch and feed a multitude. To take mud and restore sight. To take three spikes and a wooden beam and make them the hope of humanity. To take a rejected woman and make her a missionary.

There are two graves in this chapter. The first is the lonely one in the Locke Hill Cemetery. The grave of Grace Llewellen Smith. She knew not love. She knew not gratification. She knew only the pain of the chisel as it carved this epitaph into her life.

"Sleeps, but rests not.
Loved, but was loved not.
Tried to please, but pleased not.
Died as she lived—alone."

That, however, is not the only grave in this story. The second is near a water well. The tombstone? A water jug. A forgotten water jug. It has no words, but has great significance—for it is the burial place of insignificance.

1. This story is found in John 4:1-42.   2. John 4:28, 29.
3. John 4:35, Living Bible

LIVING PROOF

"Jenna, wake up, it's time to go to school."

She will hear those words a thousand times in her life. But she heard them for the first time this morning.

I sat on the edge of her bed for awhile before I said them to her. To tell the truth, I didn't want to say them. I didn't want to wake her. A queer hesitancy hung over me as I sat in the early morning blackness. As I sat in the silence, I realized that my words would awaken her to a new world.

For four lightening-fast years she'd been ours, and ours alone. And now that was all going to change.

We put her to bed last night as "our girl"— exclusive property of Mommy and Daddy. Mommy and Daddy read to her, taught her, listened to her. But beginning today, someone else would, too.

Until today, it was Mommy and Daddy who wiped away the tears and put on the Band-Aids. But beginning today, someone else would, too.

I didn't want to wake her.

Until today, her life was essentially us—Mom, Dad, and baby sister Andrea. Today that life would grow—new friends, a teacher. Her world was this house—her room, her toys, her swing set. Today her world would expand. She would enter the winding halls of education—painting, reading, calculating . . . becoming.

I didn't want to wake her. Not because of the school. It's a fine one. Not because I don't want her to learn. Heaven knows I want her to grow, to read, to mature. Not because she doesn't want to go. School has been all she can talk about for the last week!

No, I didn't want to wake her up because I didn't want to give her up.

But I woke her anyway. I interrupted her childhood with the inevitable proclamation, "Jenna, wake up . . . it's time to go to school."

It took me forever to get dressed. Denalyn saw me moping around and heard me humming, "Sunrise, Sunset" and said, "You'll never make it through her wedding." She's right.

We took her to school in two cars so that I could go directly to work. I asked Jenna to ride with me. I thought I should give her a bit of fatherly assurance. As it turned out, I was the one needing assurance.

For one dedicated to the craft of words, I found very few to share with her. I told her to enjoy herself. I told her to obey her teacher. I told her, "If you get lonely or afraid, tell your teacher to call me and I'll come and get you. "Okay," she smiled. Then she asked if she could listen to a tape with kids' music. "Okay," I said.

So while she sang songs, I swallowed lumps. I watched her as she sang. She looked big. Her little neck stretched as high as it could to look over the dash. Her eyes were hungry and bright. Her hands were folded in her lap. Her feet, wearing brand new turquoise and pink tennis shoes, barely extended over the seat.

> Is this the little girl I carried?
> Is this the little boy at play?
> I don't remember growing older.
> When did they?
>
> When did she get to be a beauty?
> When did he grow to be so tall?
> Wasn't it yesterday when they were small?
>
> Sunrise, sunset; sunrise, sunset;
> Swiftly fly the days.[1]

"Denalyn was right," I mumbled to myself, "I'll never make it through the wedding."

What is she thinking? I wondered. *Does she know how tall this ladder of education is that she will begin climbing this morning?*

No, she didn't. But I did. How many chalkboards will those eyes see? How many books will those hands hold? How many teachers will those feet follow and—gulp—imitate?

Were it within my power, I would have, at that very instant, assembled all the hundreds of teachers, instructors, coaches, and tutors that she would have over the next eighteen years and announced, "This is no normal student. This is my child. Be careful with her!"

As I parked and turned off the engine, my big girl became small again. But it was a voice of a very little girl that broke the silence. "Daddy, I don't want to get out."

I looked at her. The eyes that had been bright were now fearful. The lips that had been singing were now trembling.

I fought a Herculean urge to grant her request. Everything within me wanted to say, "Okay, let's forget it all and get out of here." For a brief, eternal moment I considered kidnaping my own daughters, grabbing my wife, and escaping these horrid paws of progress to live forever in the Himalayas.

But I knew better. I knew it was time. I knew it was right. And I knew she would be fine. But I never knew it would be so hard to say, "Honey, you'll be all right. Come on, I'll carry you."

And she was all right. One step into the classroom and the cat of curiosity pounced on her. And I walked away. I gave her up. Not much. And not as much as I will have to in the future. But I gave her up as much as I could today.

As I was walking back to my truck, a verse pounced on me. It was a passage I'd studied before. Today's events took it from black-and-white theology to technicolor reality.

"What, then, shall we say in response to this? If God is for us, who can be against us? He who did not spare his own Son, but *gave him up for us all*—how will he not also, along with him, graciously give us all things?"[2]

Is that how you felt, God? Is what I felt this morning anything like what you felt when you gave up your son?

If so, it explains so much. It explains the proclamation of the angels to the shepherds outside Bethlehem. (A proud father was announcing the birth of a son.)

It explains the voice at Jesus' baptism, "This is my son. . . ." (You did what I wanted to do, but couldn't.)

It explains the transfiguration of Moses and Elijah on the mountain top. (You sent them to encourage him.)

And it explains how your heart must have ached as you heard the cracking voice of your son, "Father, take this cup away."

I was releasing Jenna into a safe environment with a compassionate teacher who stood ready to wipe away any tears. You released Jesus into a hostile arena with a cruel soldier who turned the back of your son into raw meat.

I said good-bye to Jenna knowing she would make friends, laugh, and draw pictures. You said good-bye to Jesus knowing he would be spat upon, laughed at, and killed.

I gave up my child fully aware that were she to need me I would be at her side in a heartbeat. You said good-bye to your son fully aware that when he would need you the most, when his cry of despair would roar through the heavens, you would sit in silence. The angels, though positioned, would hear no command from you. Your son, though in anguish, would feel no comfort from your hands.

"He gave his best," Paul reasons, "why should we doubt his love?"

Before the day was over, I sat in silence a second time. This time, not beside my daughter, but before my Father. This time not sad over what I had to give, but grateful for what I'd already received—living proof that God does care.

1. "Sunrise, Sunset" (Jerry Bock, Sheldon Harnick), © 1964 — Alley Music Corp. and Trio Music Co. Inc. All rights reserved. Used by permission.   2. Romans 8:31, 32 (emphasis, mine)

FLAMING TORCHES AND LIVING PROMISES

Doubt. He's a nosey neighbor. He's an unwanted visitor. He's an obnoxious guest. Just when you were all prepared for a weekend of relaxation . . . just when you pulled off your work clothes and climbed into your Bermuda shorts . . . just when you unfolded the lawn chair and sat down with a magazine and a glass of iced tea . . . his voice interrupts your thoughts.

"Hey, Bob. Got a few minutes? I've got a few questions. I don't mean to be obnoxious, Bob, but how can you believe that a big God could ever give a hoot about you? Don't you think you are being presumptuous in thinking God wants you in heaven?

"You may think you are on pretty good terms with the man upstairs, but haven't you forgotten that business trip in Atlanta? You think he won't call your cards on that one?

"How do you know God gives a flip about you anyway?"

Got a neighbor like this?

He'll pester you. He'll irritate you. He'll criticize your judgment. He'll kick the stool out from under you and refuse to help you up. He'll tell you not to believe in the invisible yet offer no answer for the inadequacy of the visible.

He's a mealymouthed, two-faced liar who deals from the bottom of the deck. His aim is not to convince you but to confuse you. He doesn't offer solutions, he only raises questions.

Don't let him fool you. Though he may speak the current jargon, he is no newcomer. His first seeds of doubt were sown in the Garden of Eden in the heart of Eve.

There she sat, enjoying the trees, sipping on a mint julep and catching a few rays when she noticed a pair of beady eyes peering over the shrubs.

After a little small talk, he positioned himself between Eve and the sun and cast his first shadow of a doubt. "Did God really say, 'You must not eat from any tree in the garden?' "[1]

No anger. No picket signs. No "God is dead" demonstrations. Just questions.

Had any visits from this fellow lately? If you find yourself going to church in order to be saved and not because you are saved, then you've been listening to him. If you find yourself doubting if God could forgive you *again* for *that*, you've been sold some snake oil. If you are more cynical about Christians than sincere about Christ, then guess who came to dinner.

I suggest you put a lock on your gate. I suggest you post a "Do Not Enter" sign on your door. I also suggest that you take a look at an encounter between a fitful doubter and a faithful God.

Abraham, or Abram as he was known at the time, was finding God's promises about as easy to swallow as a chicken bone. The promise? That his descendants would be as numerous as the stars. The problem? No son. "No problem," came God's response.

Abraham looked over at his wife Sarah as she shuffled by in her gown and slippers with the aid of a walker. The chicken bone stuck for a few minutes but eventually slid down his throat.

Just as he was turning away to invite Sarah to a candlelight dinner he heard promise number two.

"Abram."

"Yes, Lord?"

"All this land will be yours."

Imagine God telling you that your children will someday own Fifth Avenue, and you will understand Abram's hesitation.

"On that one, Father, I need a little help."

And a little help was given.

It's a curious scene.

Twilight. The sky is a soft blue ceiling with starry diamonds. The air is cool. The animals in the pasture are quiet. The trees are silhouettes. Abram dozes under a tree. His sleep is fitful.

It's as if God is allowing Abram's doubt to run its course. In his dreams Abram is forced to face the lunacy of it all. The voices of doubt speak convincingly.

How do I know God is with me?

What if this is all a hoax?

How do you know that is God who is speaking?

The thick and dreadful darkness of doubt.

The same darkness you feel when you sit on a polished pew in a funeral chapel and listen to the obituary of the one you love more than life.

The same darkness that you feel when you hear the words, "The tumor is malignant. We have to operate."

The same darkness that falls upon you when you realize you just lost your temper . . . again.

The same darkness you feel when you realize that the divorce you never wanted is final.

The same darkness into which Jesus screamed, "My God, my God, why have you forsaken me?"

Appropriate words. For when we doubt, God seems very far away.

Which is exactly why he chose to draw so near.

God had told Abram to take three animals, cut them in half, and arrange the halves facing each other. To us the command is mysterious. To Abram, it wasn't. He'd seen the ceremony before. He'd participated in it. He'd sealed many covenants by walking through the divided carcasses and stating, "May what has happened to these animals happen also to me if I fail to uphold my word."[2]

That is why his heart must have skipped a beat when he saw the lights in the darkness passing between the carcasses. The soft golden glow from the coals in the firepot and the courageous flames from the torch. What did they mean?

The invisible God had drawn near to make his immovable promise. "To your descendants I give this land."[3]

And though God's people often forgot their God, God didn't forget them. He kept his word. The land became theirs.

God didn't give up. He never gives up.

When Joseph was dropped into a pit by his own brothers, God didn't give up.

When Moses said, "Here I am, send Aaron," God didn't give up.

When the delivered Israelites wanted Egyptian slavery instead of milk and honey, God didn't give up.

When Aaron was making a false god at the very moment Moses was with the true God, God didn't give up.

When only two of the ten spies thought the Creator was powerful enough to deliver the created, God didn't give up.

When Samson whispered to Delilah, when Saul roared after David, when David schemed against Uriah, God didn't give up.

When God's word lay forgotten and man's idols stood glistening, God didn't give up.

When the children of Israel were taken into captivity, God didn't give up.

He could have given up. He could have turned his back. He could have walked away from the wretched mess, but he didn't.

He didn't give up.

When he became flesh and was the victim of an assassination attempt before he was two years old, he didn't give up.

When the people from his own home town tried to push him over a cliff, he didn't give up.

When his brothers ridiculed him, he didn't give up.

When he was accused of blaspheming God by people who didn't fear God, he didn't give up.

When Peter worshiped him at the supper and cursed him at the fire, he didn't give up.

When people spat in his face, he didn't spit back. When the bystanders slapped him, he didn't slap them. When a whip ripped his sides, he didn't turn and command the awaiting angels to stuff that whip down that soldier's throat.

And when human hands fastened the divine hands to a cross with spikes, it wasn't the soldiers who held the hands of Jesus steady. It was God who held them steady. For those wounded hands were the same invisible hands that had carried the firepot and the torch two thousand years earlier. They were the same hands that had brought light into Abraham's thick and dreadful darkness. They had come to do it again.

So, the next time that obnoxious neighbor walks in, escort him out. Out to the hill. Out to Calvary. Out to the cross where, with holy blood, the hand that carried the flame wrote the promise, "God would give up his only son before he'd give up on you."

1. Genesis 3:1   2. Jeremiah 34:18   3. Genesis 15:18

ANGELIC MESSAGES

I had every right to be angry. If you'd had a week like mine, you would have been angry, too.

My problems began on Sunday night. I was still living in Brazil and was taking some relatives to southern Brazil to see the Iguaçú Falls. A canceled flight left us stranded several hours in the Sao Paulo airport. No warning. No explanation. Just a notification as we were landing that the plane we were going to catch was going nowhere. If we wanted, we could wait two hours and catch another one.

"If we wanted!" Grrrr.

When we got to our hotel, it was raining. It rained until the day we left.

Determined to record the falls, I carried my video camera for one mile through a rainstorm. I don't mean a drizzle or a sprinkle or a shower, I mean a blinding downpour. When I reached the falls, I realized I had left the camera turned on for the previous hour and filmed the inside of the camera bag and run down the battery.

When I got back to the hotel, I realized that the rain had ruined the camera. How much ruin? Three hundred dollars' worth of ruin. That was Wednesday. The week wasn't over yet.

When I got back to Rio I found out that Denalyn had told her family that we were going to spend the upcoming Christmas with them. I had already told my family that we were going to spend the holidays with them.

Thursday was the clincher. Denalyn called me at home. Our car had broken down. The car that the car dealer promised was in great shape. The car that the car dealer promised was worth the extra money. The car that the car dealer had sworn was trouble-free. It broke down. Downtown. Again. On my day off.

I walked to the shopping center. I spoke to no one. No one dared to speak to me.

I sat in the car and tried to start it. No luck. When I turned the key in the ignition all I could hear were the promises of the car dealer and the jingle of the mechanic's cash register. I spent an hour tinkering with a broken-down car in a parking lot.

Finally I called the mechanic. The tow truck was busy. Could I wait a few minutes? In Brazil, the word *minutes* can better be translated "years." So I waited. And I waited. And I waited. My children grew up and had children of their own and still I was waiting.

Finally, as the sun was setting, the truck appeared. "Put it in neutral," I was instructed. As I climbed in the car I thought, *Might as well try it one more time.* I turned the key in the ignition. Guess what? You got it. It started.

That should be good news. It was, until I saw the driver of the tow truck in no hurry to leave. He wanted to be paid. "For what?" I implored. "Was it my fault your car started?" he replied. It's a good thing I didn't know how to say "smart aleck" in Portuguese. So I paid him for watching me start my car.

I immediately drove the car to the mechanic. As I drove, two devils came and perched on my shoulders. The fact that I couldn't see them didn't make them any less real. I could hear them—they spoke the language of the Liar.

One was anger. If there was anything I wasn't mad at by this point, he took care of that. My list of offenses was long and ugly.

The other was self-pity. Boy, did he find a listening ear. Not only had I had a bad week, he reminded me that I had been plagued with a bad life! Born with the handicap of freckles and red hair. Always too slow for track. Never elected "most likely to succeed." And now, a missionary suffering on foreign soil.

Anger in one ear and self-pity in the other . . . if I hadn't seen him, who knows what I would have done.

He didn't look like an angel. In fact, he looked like anything but an angel. But I know he was an angel, for only angels bring that type of a message.

He knocked on my car window.

"Trocadinho, Senhor?" ("Do you have any spare change, sir?")

He was, at most, nine years old. Shirtless. Barefooted. Dirty. So dirty, I couldn't tell if he was wearing shorts or not. His hair was matted. His skin was crusty. I rolled down the window. The voices on my shoulders became silent.

"What's your name?" I asked.

"José."

I looked over at the sidewalk. Two other street orphans were walking towards the cars behind me. They were naked except for ragged gym shorts.

"Are they your brothers?" I asked.

"No, just friends."

"Have you collected much money today?"

He opened a dirty hand full of coins. Enough money, perhaps, for a soft drink.

I reached in my wallet and pulled out the equivalent to a dollar. His eyes brightened. Mine watered. The light changed and the cars behind me honked. As I drove away I saw him running to tell his friends what he had received.

The voices on my shoulders didn't dare say a word. Nor did I. The three of us drove in shameful silence.

I figured I had said enough. And God had heard every word.

What if God had responded to my grumblings? What if he'd heeded my complaints? He could have. He could have answered my carelessly mumbled prayers. And had he chosen to do so, a prototype of the result had just appeared at my door.

"Don't want to mess with airlines? This boy doesn't have that problem. Frustrated with your video camera? That's one headache this boy doesn't have. He may have to worry about tonight's dinner, but he doesn't have to worry about video cameras. And family? I'm sure this orphan would gladly take one of your families if you are too busy to appreciate them. And cars? Yes, they are a hassle, aren't they? You should try this boy's mode of transportation— bare feet."

God sent the boy with a message. And the point the boy made was razor-sharp.

"You cry over spilled champagne."

Ouch.

"Your complaints are not over the lack of necessities but the abundance of benefits. You bellyache over the frills, not the basics; over benefits, not essentials. The source of your problems is your blessings."

José gave me a lot for my dollar; he gave me a lesson on gratitude.

Gratitude. More aware of what you have than what you don't. Recognizing the treasure in the simple—a child's hug, fertile soil, a golden sunset. Relishing in the comfort of the common—a warm bed, a hot meal, a clean shirt.

And no one has more reason to be grateful than does the one who has been reminded of God's gift by one of God's angels. I was. And so was Franciszek Gajowniczek. His story is moving.

It's difficult to find beauty in death. It's even more difficult to find beauty in a death camp. Especially Auschwitz. Four million Jews died there in World War II. A half-ton of human hair is still preserved. The showers that sprayed poison gas still stand.

But for all the ugly memories of Auschwitz there is one of beauty. It's the memory Gajowniczek has of Maximilian Kolbe.

In February, 1941, Kolbe was incarcerated at Auschwitz. He was a Franciscan priest. In the harshness of the slaughterhouse he maintained the gentleness of Christ. He shared his food. He gave up his bunk. He prayed for his captors. He was soon given the nickname "Saint of Auschwitz."

In July of that same year there was an escape from the prison. It was the custom at Auschwitz to kill ten prisoners for every one who escaped. All the prisoners would be gathered in the courtyard and the commandant would randomly select ten names from the roll book. These victims would be immediately taken to a cell where they would receive no food or water until they died.

The commandant begins calling the names. At each selection another prisoner steps forward to fill the sinister quota. The tenth name he calls is Gajowniczek.

As the SS officers check the numbers of the condemned, one of the condemned begins to sob. "My wife and my children," he weeps.

The officers turn as they hear movement among the prisoners. The guards raise their rifles. The dogs tense, anticipating a command to attack. A prisoner has left his row and is pushing his way to the front.

It is Kolbe. No fear on his face. No hesitancy in his step. The capo shouts at him to stop or be shot. "I want to talk to the commander," he says calmly. For some reason the officer doesn't club or kill him. Kolbe stops a few paces from the commandant, removes his hat and looks the German officer in the eye.

"Herr Kommandant, I wish to make a request, please."

That no one shot him is a miracle.

"I want to die in the place of this prisoner." He points at the sobbing Gajowniczek. The audacious request is presented without stammer.

"I have no wife and children. Besides, I am old and not good for anything. He's in better condition." Kolbe knew well the Nazi mentality.

"Who are you?" the officer asks.

"A Catholic priest."

The block is stunned. The commandant, uncharacteristically speechless. After a moment, he barks, "Request granted."

Prisoners were never allowed to speak. Gajowniczek says,

"I could only thank him with my eyes. I was stunned and could hardly grasp what was going on. The immensity of it: I, the condemned, am to live and someone else willingly and voluntarily offers his life for me—a stranger. Is this some dream?"

The Saint of Auschwitz outlived the other nine. In fact, he didn't die of thirst or starvation. He died only after the camp doctor injected phenol into his heart. It was August 14, 1941.

Gajowniczek survived the Holocaust. He made his way back to his hometown. Every year, however, he goes back to Auschwitz. Every August 14 he goes back to say thank you to the man who died in his place.

In his back yard there is a plaque. A plaque he carved with his own hands. A tribute to Maximilian Kolbe—the man who died so he could live.[1]

There are times that it takes an angel to remind us about what we have.

There aren't very many similarities between Franciszek Gajowniczek and Max Lucado. We speak two different languages. We salute two different flags. We know two different homelands. But we do have three things in common.

We both had an angel set us free from a prison. We both had a Jewish teacher die in our place. And we both learned that what we already have is far greater than anything we might want.

1. This story is adpted from the book *A Man for Others* by Patricia Treece.

REMEMBER

On the evening of the first day of the week,
when the disciples were together,
with the doors locked for fear of the Jews. . ."
John 20:19

The church of Jesus Christ began with a group of frightened men in a second-floor room in Jerusalem.

Though trained and taught, they didn't know what to say. Though they'd marched with him for three years, they now sat . . . afraid. They were timid soldiers, reluctant warriors, speechless messengers.

Their most courageous act was to get up and lock the door.

Some looked out the window, some looked at the wall, some looked at the floor, but all looked inside themselves.

And well they should, for it was an hour of self-examination. All their efforts seemed so futile. Nagging their memories were the promises they'd made but not kept. When the Roman soldiers took Jesus, Jesus' followers took off. With the very wine of the covenant on their breath and the bread of his sacrifice in their bellies, they fled.

All those boasts of bravado? All those declarations of devotion? They lay broken and shattered at the gate of Gethsemane's garden.

We don't know where the disciples went when they fled the garden, but we do know what they took: a memory. They took a heart-stopping memory of a man who called himself no less than God in the flesh. And they couldn't get him out of their minds. Try as they might to lose him in the crowd, they couldn't forget him. If they saw a leper, they thought of his compassion. If they heard a storm, they would remember the day he silenced one. If they saw a child, they would think of the day he held one. And if they saw a lamb being carried to the temple, they would remember his face streaked with blood and his eyes flooded with love.

No, they couldn't forget him. As a result, they came back. And, as a result, the church of our Lord began with a group of frightened men in an upper room.

Sound familiar? Things haven't changed much in two thousand years, have they? How many churches today find themselves paralyzed in the upper room?

How many congregations have just enough religion to come together, but not enough passion to go out? If the doors aren't locked, they might as well be.

Upper room futility. A little bit of faith but very little fire.

> "Sure, we're doing our part to reach the world. Why, just last year we mailed ten correspondence courses. We're anticipating a response any day now."

> "You bet we care that the world is reached! We send $150 a month to . . . uh, well . . . ol' what's-his-name down there in . . . uh, well, oh, I forget the place, but . . . we pray for it often."

> "World hunger? Why, that's high on our priority list! In fact, we have plans to plan a planning session. At least, that is what we are planning to do."

Good people. Lots of ideas. Plenty of good intentions. Budgets. Meetings. Words. Promises. But while all this is going on, the door remains locked and the story stays a secret.

You don't turn your back on Christ, but you don't turn toward him either. You don't curse his name, but neither do you praise it. You know you should do something, but you're not sure what. You know you should come together, but you're not sure why.

Upper room futility. Confused ambassadors behind locked doors. What will it take to unlock them? What will it take to ignite the fire? What will it take to restore the first century passion? What will have to happen before the padlocks of futility tumble from our doors and are trampled under the feet of departing disciples?

More training? That's part of it. Better strategies? That would help. A greater world vision? Undoubtedly. More money? That's imperative. A greater dependence on the Holy Spirit? Absolutely.

But in the midst of these items there is one basic ingredient that cannot be overlooked. There is one element so vital that its absence insures our failure. What is needed to get us out is exactly what got the apostles out.

Picture the scene. Peter, John, James. They came back. Banking on some zany possibility that the well of forgiveness still had a few drops, they came back. Daring to dream that the master had left them some word, some plan, some direction, they came back.

But little did they know, their wildest dream wasn't wild enough. Just as someone mumbles, "It's no use," they hear a noise. They hear a voice.

"Peace be with you."[1]

Every head lifted. Every eye turned. Every mouth dropped open. Someone looked at the door.

It was still locked.

It was a moment the apostles would never forget, a story they would never cease to tell. The stone of the tomb was not enough to keep him *in*. The walls of the room were not enough to keep him *out*.

The one betrayed sought his betrayers. What did he say to them? Not "What a bunch of flops!" Not "I told you so." No "Where-were-you-when-

I-needed-you?'' speeches. But simply one phrase, "Peace be with you." The very thing they didn't have was the very thing he offered: peace.

It was too good to be true! So amazing was the appearance that some were saying, "Pinch me, I'm dreaming" even at the ascension.[2] No wonder they returned to Jerusalem with great joy![3] No wonder they were always in the temple praising God![4]

A transformed group stood beside a transformed Peter as he announced some weeks later: "Therefore let all Israel be assured of this: God has made this Jesus, whom you crucified, both Lord and Christ."[5]

No timidity in his words. No reluctance. About three thousand people believed his message.

The apostles sparked a movement. The people became followers of the death-conqueror. They couldn't hear enough or say enough about him. People began to call them "Christ-ians." Christ was their model, their message. They preached "Jesus Christ and him crucified," not for the lack of another topic, but because they couldn't exhaust this one.

What unlocked the doors of the apostles' hearts?

Simple. They saw Jesus. They encountered the Christ. Their sins collided with their Savior and their Savior won! What lit the boiler of the apostles was a red-hot conviction that the very one who should have sent them to hell went to hell for them and came back to tell about it.

A lot of things would happen to them over the next few decades. Many nights would be spent away from home. Hunger would gnaw at their bellies. Rain would soak their skin. Stones would bruise their bodies. Shipwrecks, lashings, martyrdom. But there was a scene in the repertoire of memories that caused them to never look back: the betrayed coming back to find his betrayers; not to scourge them, but to send them. Not to criticize them for forgetting, but to commission them to remember. *Remember* that he who was dead is alive and they who were guilty have been forgiven.

Think about the first time you ever saw him. Think about your first encounter with the Christ. Robe yourself in that moment. Resurrect the relief. Recall the purity. Summon forth the passion. Can you remember?

I can. 1965. A red-headed ten-year-old with a tornado of freckles sits in a Bible class on a Wednesday night. What I remember of the class are scenes—school desks with initials carved in them. A blackboard. A dozen or so kids, some listening, some not. A teacher wearing a suit coat too tight to button around his robust belly.

He is talking about Jesus. He is explaining the cross. I know I had heard it before, but that night I heard it for sure. "You can't save yourself, you need a savior." I can't explain why it connected that night as opposed to another, but it did. He simply articulated what I was beginning to understand—I was lost—and he explained what I needed—a redeemer. From that night on, my heart belonged to Jesus.

Many would argue that a ten-year-old is too young for such a decision. And they may be right. All I know is that I never made a more earnest decision in my life. I didn't know much about God, but what I knew was enough. I knew I wanted to go to heaven. And I knew I couldn't do it alone.

No one had to tell me to be happy. No one had to tell me to tell others. They couldn't keep me quiet. I told all my friends at school. I put a bumper sticker on my bicycle. And though I'd never read 2 Corinthians 4:13, I knew what it meant. "I believed; therefore I have spoken." Pardon truly received is pardon powerfully proclaimed.

There is a direct correlation between the accuracy of our memory and the effectiveness of our mission. If we are not teaching people how to be saved, it is perhaps because we have forgotten the tragedy of being lost! If we're not teaching the message of forgiveness, it may be because we don't remember what it was like to be guilty. And if we're not preaching the cross, it could be that we've subconsciously decided that—God forbid—somehow we don't need it.

In what was perhaps the last letter Paul ever wrote, he begged Timothy not to forget. In a letter written within earshot of the sharpening of the blade that would sever his head, he urged Timothy to remember. "Remember Jesus Christ . . ."[6] You can almost picture the old warrior smiling as he wrote the words. "Remember Jesus Christ, raised from the dead, descended from David. This is my gospel. . . ."

When times get hard, remember Jesus. When people don't listen, remember Jesus. When tears come, remember Jesus. When disappointment is your bedpartner, remember Jesus. When fear pitches his tent in your front yard. When death looms, when anger singes, when shame weighs heavily. Remember Jesus.

Remember holiness in tandem with humanity. Remember the sick who were healed with calloused hands. Remember the dead called from the grave with a Galilean accent. Remember the eyes of God that wept human tears. And, most of all, remember this descendant of David who beat the hell out of death.

Can you still remember? Are you still in love with him? Remember, Paul begged, remember Jesus. Before you remember anything, remember him. If you forget anything, don't forget him.

Oh, but how quickly we forget. So much happens through the years. So many changes within. So many alterations without. And, somewhere, back there, we leave him. We don't turn away from him . . . we just don't take him with us. Assignments come. Promotions come. Budgets are made. Kids are born, and the Christ . . . the Christ is forgotten.

Has it been a while since you stared at the heavens in speechless amazement? Has it been a while since you realized God's divinity and your carnality?

If it has, then you need to know something. He is still there. He hasn't left. Under all those papers and books and reports and years. In the midst of all those voices and faces and memories and pictures, he is still there.

Do yourself a favor. Stand before him again. Or, better, allow him to stand before you. Go into your upper room and wait. Wait until he comes. And when he appears, don't leave. Run your fingers over his feet. Place your hand in the pierced side. And look into those eyes. Those same eyes that melted the gates of hell and sent the demons scurrying and Satan running. Look at them as they look at you. You'll never be the same.

A man is never the same after he simultaneously sees his utter despair and Christ's unbending grace. To see the despair without the grace is suicidal. To see the grace without the despair is upper room futility. But to see them both is conversion.

1. John 20:19   2. Matthew 28:17   3. Luke 24:52   4. Luke 24:53   5. Acts 2:36   6. 2 Timothy 2:8

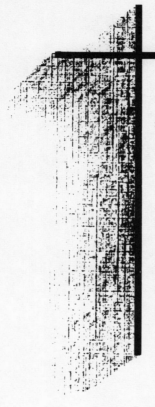

ANCHOR POINT 2

MY
FAILURES
ARE NOT
FATAL

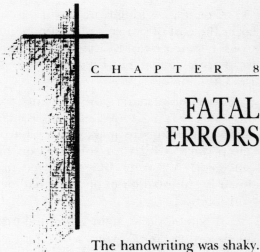

FATAL ERRORS

The handwriting was shaky. The stationery was lined loose-leaf paper. The ink was black and the tone desperate. The note was dated February 6, 1974 and was addressed to the U.S. government.

"I am sending ten dollars for blankets I stole while in World War II. My mind could not rest. Sorry I'm late." It was signed, "an ex-GI." Then there was this postscript, "I want to be ready to meet God."

This recruit was not alone in his guilt. His letter is one of literally tons of letters that have been sent to the U.S. government since it began collecting and storing the letters in 1811. Since that time $3,500,000 has been deposited in what is called the Conscience Fund.

An average of $45,000 per year is received. The biggest year was 1950 in which $350,000 was collected.

One man writing from Brazil sent fifty dollars to cover the cost of two pair of cavalry boots, two pair of trousers, one case of KC rations and thirty pounds of fresh frozen meat he stole from the army between 1943 and 1946.

In some instances the amounts are small, only the remorse is big. One Colorado woman sent in two eight-cent stamps to make up for having used one stamp twice (which for some reason had not been canceled.) A former IRS employee mailed in one dollar for four ballpoint pens she had never returned to the office.

A Salem, Ohio, man submitted one dollar with the following note, "When a boy, I put a few pennies on the railroad track and the train flattened them. I also used a dime or a quarter in a silver-coating experiment in high school. I understand there is a law against defacing our money. I have not seen it but I desire to be a law-abiding citizen."

Anxiety over a thirty-year-old mistake? Regret over mashed pennies? A guilty conscience because of ballpoint pens? If the struggle to have a clean conscience wasn't so common, the letters would be funny. But the struggle *is* common.

What do you do with your failures? Our mistakes come to us as pebbles; small stones that serve as souvenirs of our stumbles. We carry them in our hands, and soon our hands are full. We put them in our pockets, and soon our pockets bulge. We place them in a bag and put it over our shoulder; the burlap scratches and chaps. And soon the bag of yesterday's failures is so heavy, we drag it.

Here are some failures that have been drug into my office.

Unfaithfulness. He wanted to try again. She said, "No way." He wanted a second chance. She said, "You blew your chance." He admitted that he made a mistake by seeing another woman. He sees now that the mistake was fatal to his marriage.

Homosexuality. His wrists bore the scars of a suicide attempt. His arms had tracks from countless needles. His eyes reflected the spirit of one hell-bent on self-destruction. His words were those of a prisoner grimly resigned to the judge's sentence. "I'm gay. My dad says I'm a queer. I guess he's right."

Division. A church leadership demanded submission. A membership demanded a louder voice. It was a bomb waiting to explode. The eruption resulted in a half-empty building of walking wounded.

Immorality. She came to church with a pregnant womb and a repentant spirit. "I can't have a child," she pleaded. "We'll find a home for it," she was assured. She agreed. Then she changed her mind. Her boyfriend funded the abortion. "Can God ever forgive me?" she asked.

Nothing drags more stubbornly than a sack of failures.

Could you do it all over again, you'd do it differently. You'd be a different person. You'd be more patient. You'd control your tongue. You'd finish what you started. You'd turn the other cheek instead of slapping his. You'd get married first. You wouldn't marry at all. You'd be honest. You'd resist the temptation. You'd run with a different crowd.

But you can't. And as many times as you tell yourself, "What's done is done," what you did can't be undone.

That's part of what Paul meant when he said, "The wages of sin is death".[1] He didn't say, "The wages of sin is a bad mood." Or, "The wages of sin is a hard day." Nor, "The wages of sin is depression." Read it again. "The wages of sin is death." Sin is fatal.

Can anything be done with it?

Your therapist tells you to talk about it. So you do. You pull the bag into his office and pour the rocks out on his floor and analyze each one. And it's helpful. It feels good to talk and he's nice. But when the hour is up, you still have to carry the bag out with you.

Your friends tell you not to feel bad. "Everyone slumps a bit in this world," they say. "Not very comforting," you say.

Feel-great-about-life rallies tell you to ignore the thing and be happy! Which works—until you wipe the fog off your mirror and take an honest look. Then you see, it's still there.

Legalists tell you to work the weight off. A candle for every rock. A prayer for every pebble. Sounds logical. but what if I run out of time? Or what if I didn't count correctly? You panic.

What *do* you do with the stones from life's stumbles?

My oldest daughter, Jenna, is four years old. Some time ago she came to me with a confession.

"Daddy, I took a crayon and drew on the wall." (Kids amaze me with their honesty.)

I sat down and lifted her up into my lap and tried to be wise. "Is that a good thing to do?" I asked her.

"No."

"What does Daddy do when you write on the wall?"

"You spank me."

"What do you think Daddy should do this time?"

"Love."

Don't we all want that? Don't we all long for a father who, even though our mistakes are written all over the wall, will love us anyway? Don't we want a father who cares for us in spite of our failures?

We *do* have that type of a father. A father who is at his best when we are at our worst. A father whose grace is strongest when our devotion is weakest. If your bag is big and bulky, then you're in for some thrilling news: Your failures are not fatal.

1. Romans 6:23

CRISTO REDENTOR

Ninety feet tall. One thousand three hundred twenty tons of reinforced Brazilian tile. Positioned on a mountain a mile and one-half above sea level. It's the famous *Christ the Redeemer* statue that overlooks the city of Rio de Janeiro, Brazil.

No tourist comes to Rio without snaking up Corcovado mountain to see this looming monument. The head alone is nine feet tall. The wingspan from fingertip to fingertip—sixty-three feet.

While living in Rio, I saw the statue dozens of times. But no time was as impressive as the first.

I was a college student spending a summer in Brazil. Except for scampers across the Mexican border, this was my first trip outside the continental U.S. I had known this monument only through *National*

Geographic magazine. I was to learn that no magazine can truly capture the splendor of *Cristo Redentor.*

Below me was Rio. Seven million people swarming on the lush green mountains that crash into the bright blue Atlantic. Behind me was the *Christ the Redeemer* statue. As I looked at the towering edifice through my telephoto lens, two ironies caught my attention.

I couldn't help but notice the blind eyes. Now, I know what you are thinking—all statues have blind eyes. You are right, they do. But it's as if the sculptor of this statue intended that the eyes be blind. There are no pupils to suggest vision. There are no circles to suggest sight. There are only Little Orphan Annie openings.

I lowered my camera to my waist. *What kind of redeemer is this? Blind? Eyes fixated on the horizon, refusing to see the mass of people at its feet?*

I saw the second irony as I again raised my camera. I followed the features downward; past the strong nose, past the prominent chin, past the neck. My focus came to rest on the cloak of the statue. On the outside of the cloak there is a heart. A Valentine's heart. A simple heart.

A stone heart.

The unintended symbolism staggered me. *What kind of redeemer is this? Heart made of stone? Held together, not with passion and love, but by concrete and mortar. What kind of redeemer is this? Blind eyes and stony heart?*

I've since learned the answer to my own question: What kind of redeemer is this? Exactly the kind of redeemer most people have.

Oh, most people would not admit to having a blind redeemer with a stone heart. But take a close look.

For some, Jesus is a good luck charm. The "Rabbit's Foot Redeemer." Pocket-sized. Handy. Easily packaged. Easily understood. Easily diagramed. You can put his picture on your wall or you can stick it in your wallet as insurance. You can frame him. Dangle him from your rear view mirror or glue him to your dashboard.

His specialty? Getting you out of a jam. Need a parking place? Rub the redeemer. Need help on a quiz? Pull out the rabbit's foot. No need to have a relationship with him. No need to love him. Just keep him in your pocket next to your four-leaf clover.

For many he's an "Aladdin's Lamp Redeemer." New jobs. Pink Cadillacs. New and improved spouses. Your wish is his command. And what's more, he conveniently reenters the lamp when you don't want him around.

For others, Jesus is a "Monty Hall Redeemer." "All right, Jesus, let's make a deal. For fifty-two Sundays a year, I'll put on a costume—coat and tie, hat and hose—and I'll endure any sermon you throw at me. In exchange, you give me the grace behind pearly gate number three."

The Rabbit's Foot Redeemer. The Aladdin's Lamp Redeemer. The Monty Hall Redeemer. Few demands, no challenges. No need for sacrifice. No need for commitment.

Sightless and heartless redeemers. Redeemers without power. That's not the Redeemer of the New Testament.

Compare the blind Christ I saw in Rio to the compassionate one seen by a frightened woman early one morning in Jerusalem.[1]

It's dawn. The early morning sun stretches a golden blanket across the streets of the city. Diamonds of dew cling to blades of grass. A cat stretches as it awakens. The noises are scattered.

A rooster crows his early morning recital.

A dog barks to welcome the day.

A peddler shuffles down the street, his wares on his back.

And a young carpenter speaks in the courtyard.

Jesus sits surrounded by a horseshoe of listeners. Some nod their heads in agreement and open their hearts in obedience. They have accepted the teacher as their teacher and are learning to accept him as their Lord.

Others are curious, wanting to believe yet wary of this one whose claims so stretch the boundaries of belief.

Whether cautious or convinced, they listen keenly. They arose early. There was something about his words that was more comforting than sleep.

We don't know his topic that morning. Prayer, perhaps. Or maybe kindness or anxiety. But whatever it was, it was soon interrupted when people burst into the courtyard.

Determined, they erupt out of a narrow street and stomp toward Jesus. The listeners scramble to get out of the way. The mob is made up of religious leaders, the elders and deacons of their day. Respected and important men. And struggling to keep her balance on the crest of this angry wave is a scantily-clad woman.

Only moments before she had been in bed with a man who was not her husband. Was this how she made her living? Maybe. Maybe not. Maybe her husband was gone, her heart was lonely, the stranger's touch was warm, and before she knew it, she had done it. We don't know.

But we do know that a door was jerked open and she was yanked from a bed. She barely had time to cover her body before she was dragged into the street by two men the age of her father. What thoughts raced through her mind as she scrambled to keep her feet?

Curious neighbors stuck heads through open windows. Sleepy dogs yelped at the ruckus.

And now, with holy strides, the mob storms toward the teacher. They throw the woman in his direction. She nearly falls.

"We found this woman in bed with a man!" cries the leader. "The law says to stone her. What do you say?"

Cocky with borrowed courage, they smirk as they watch the mouse go for the cheese.

The woman searches the faces, hungry for a compassionate glance. She finds none. Instead, she sees accusation. Squinty eyes. Tight lips. Gritted teeth. Stares that sentence without seeing.

Cold, stony hearts that condemn without feeling.

She looks down and sees the rocks in their hands—the rocks of righteousness intended to stone the lust out of her. The men squeeze them so tightly that their fingertips are white. They squeeze them as if the rocks were the throat of this preacher they hate.

In her despair she looks at the Teacher. His eyes don't glare. "Don't worry," they whisper, "it's okay." And for the first time that morning she sees kindness.

When Jesus saw her, what did he see? Did he see her as a father sees his grown daughter as she walks down the wedding aisle? The father's mind races back through time watching his girl grow up again— from diapers to dolls. From classrooms to boyfriends. From the prom date to the wedding day. The father sees it all as he looks at his daughter.

As Jesus looked at this daughter, did his mind race back? Did he relive the act of forming this child in heaven? Did he see her as he had originally made her?

"Knitted together" is how the psalmist described the process of God making man.[2] Not manufactured or mass-produced, but knitted. Each thread of personality tenderly intertwined. Each string of temperament deliberately selected.

God as creator. Pensive. Excited. Inventive.

> An artist, brush on pallet, seeking the perfect shade.
>
> A composer, fingers on keyboard, listening for the exact chord.
>
> A poet, pen poised on paper, awaiting the precise word.

The Creator, the master weaver, threading
together the soul.

Each one different. No two alike. None
identical.

On earth, Jesus was an artist in a gallery of his
own paintings. He was a composer listening as the
orchestra interpreted his music. He was a poet hearing his own poetry. Yet his works of art had been
defaced. Creation after battered creation.

He had created people for splendor. They had
settled for mediocrity. He had formed them with
love. They had scarred each other with hate.

When he saw businessmen using God-given in-
teligence to feed Satan-given greed . . .

When he saw tongues he had designed to encourage used as daggers to cut . . .

When he saw hands that had been given for
holding used as weapons for hurting . . .

When he saw eyes into which he'd sprinkled joy
now burning with hatred . . .

I wonder, did it weary him to see hearts that
were stained, even discarded?

Jesus saw such a heart as he looked at this woman. Her feet were bare and muddy. Her arms hid
her chest and her hands clutched each other under
her chin. And her heart, her heart was ragged; torn
as much by her own guilt as by the mob's anger.

So, with the tenderness only a father can have,
he set out to untie the knots and repair the holes.

He begins by diverting the crowd's attention.
He draws on the ground. Everybody looks down. The

woman feels relief as the eyes of the men look away from her.

The accusers are persistent. "Tell us teacher! What do you want us to do with her?"

He could have asked why they didn't bring the man. The Law indicted him as well. He could have asked why they were suddenly blowing the dust off an old command that had sat on the shelves for centuries. But he didn't.

He just raised his head and offered an invitation, "I guess if you've never made a mistake, then you have a right to stone this woman." He looked back down and began to draw on the earth again.

Someone cleared his throat as if to speak, but no one spoke. Feet shuffled. Eyes dropped. Then thud . . . thud . . . thud . . . rocks fell to the ground.

And they walked away. Beginning with the grayest beard and ending with the blackest, they turned and left. They came as one, but they left one by one.

Jesus told the woman to look up. "Is there no one to condemn you?" He smiled as she raised her head. She saw no one, only rocks—each one a miniature tombstone to mark the burial place of a man's arrogance.

"Is there no one to condemn you?" he'd asked. *There is still one who can,* she thinks. And she turns to look at him.

What does he want? What will he do?

Maybe she expected him to scold her. Perhaps she expected him to walk away from her. I'm not sure, but I do know this: What she got, she never expected. She got a promise and a commission.

The promise: "Then neither do I condemn you."

The commission: "Go and sin no more."

The woman turns and walks into anonymity. She's never seen or heard from again. But we can be confident of one thing: On that morning in Jerusalem, she saw Jesus and Jesus saw her. And could we somehow transport her to Rio de Janeiro and let her stand at the base of the *Cristo Redentor,* I know what her response would be.

"That's not the Jesus I saw," she would say. And she would be right. For the Jesus she saw didn't have a hard heart. And the Jesus that saw her didn't have blind eyes.

However, if we could somehow transport her to Calvary and let her stand at the base of the cross . . . you know what she would say. "That's him," she would whisper. "That's him."

She would recognize his hands. The only hands that had held no stones that day were his. And on this day they still hold no stones. She would recognize his voice. It's raspier and weaker, but the words are the same, "Father, forgive them. . . ." And she would recognize his eyes. How could she ever forget those eyes? Clear and tear-filled. Eyes that saw her not as she was, but as she was intended to be.

1. John 8:1-11   2. Psalm 139:13

CHAPTER 10

THE GOLDEN GOBLET

Flames leap from the hill. Pillows of smoke float upward. Orange tongues crack and pop.

From the midst of the blaze comes a yell—the protest of a prisoner as the dungeon door is locked; the roar of a lion as he feels the heat of the burning jungle.

The cry of a lost son as he looks for his father.

"My God, my God, why have you forsaken me?"

The words ricochet from star to star, crashing into the chamber of the King. Couriers from a bloody battlefield, they stumble into the King's presence. Bruised and broken, they plea for help, for relief.

The soldiers of the King prepare to attack. They mount their steeds and position their shields. They draw their swords.

But the King is silent. It is the hour for which he has planned. He knows his course of action. He has awaited those words since the beginning—since the first poison was smuggled into the kingdom.

It came camouflaged. It came in a golden cup with a long stem. It was in the flavor of fruit. It came, not in the hands of a king, but the hands of a prince—the prince of the shadows.

Until this moment there had been no reason to hide in the Garden. The King walked with his children and the children knew their King. There were no secrets. There were no shadows.

Then the prince of shadows entered the Garden. He had to hide himself. He was too ugly, too repulsive. Craters marred his face. So he came in darkness. He came encircled in ebony. He was completely hidden; only his voice could be heard.

"Taste it," he whispered, holding the goblet before her. "It's sweet with wisdom."

The daughter heard the voice and turned. She was intrigued. Her eyes had never seen a shadow. There was something tantalizing about his hiddeness.

The King watched. His army knew the prince of shadows would be no contest for their mighty legion. Eagerly, they awaited the command to attack.

But no command was given.

"The choice is hers," the King instructed. "If she turns to us for help, that is your command to deliver her. If she doesn't turn, if she doesn't look to me—don't go. The choice is hers."

The daughter stared at the goblet. Rubies embedded in gold filigree invited her touch. Wine wooed her to taste. She reached out and took the cup and drank the poison. Her eyes never looked up.

The venom rushed through her, distorting her vision, scarring her skin, and twisting her heart. She ducked into the shadow of the prince.

Suddenly, she was lonely. She missed the intimacy she was made to know. Yet rather than return to the King, she chose to lure another away from him. She replenished the goblet and offered it to the son.

Once again the army snapped into position. Once again they listened for the command of the King. His words were the same. "If he looks to me, then rush to him. If he doesn't, then don't go. The choice is his."

The daughter placed the goblet into the hands of the son. "It's all right," she assured. "It's sweet." The son looked at the delight that danced in her eyes. Behind her stood a silhouetted figure.

"Who is he?" the son asked.

"Drink it," she insisted. Her voice was husky with desire.

The goblet was cold against Adam's lips. The liquid burned his innocence. "More?" he requested as he ran his finger through the dregs on the bottom and put it to his mouth.

The soldiers looked to their King for instructions. His eyes were moist.

"Bring me your sword!" The general dismounted and stepped quickly toward the throne. He extended the unsheathed blade before the King.

The King didn't take it, he merely touched it. As the tip of his finger encountered the top of the sword, the iron grew orange with heat. It grew brighter and brighter until it blazed.

The general held the fiery sword and awaited the King's command. It came in the form of an edict.

"Their choice will be honored. Where there is poison, there will be death. Where there are goblets, there will be fire. Let it be done."

The general galloped to the Garden and took his post at the gate. The flaming sword proclaimed that the kingdom of light would never again be darkened by the passing of shadows. The King hated the shadows. He hated them because in the shadows the children could not see their King. The King hated the goblets. He hated them because they made the children forget the Father.

But outside the Garden, the circle of the shadow grew larger and more empty goblets littered the ground. More faces were disfigured. More eyes saw distortedly. More souls were twisted. Purity was forgotten and all sight of the King was lost. No one remembered that once there was a kingdom without shadows.

In their hands were the goblets of selfishness.

On their lips was the litany of the liar. "Taste it, it's sweet."

And, true to the words of the King, where there was poison, there was death. Where there were goblets, there was fire. Until the day the King sent his Prince.

The same fire that ignited the sword now lit a candle and placed it amidst the shadows.

His arrival, like that of the goblet-bearer, did not go unnoticed.

"A star!" was how his coming was announced. "A bright light in a dark sky." A diamond glittering in the dirt.

"Burn brightly, my Son," whispered the King.

Many times the Prince of Light was offered the goblet. Many times it came in the hands of those who'd abandoned the King. "Just a taste, my friend?" With anguish Jesus would look into the eyes of those who tried to tempt him. What is this poison that would make a prisoner try to kill the one who came to release him?

The goblet still bore the seductive flavor of promised power and pleasure. But to the Son of Light its odor was vile. The very sight of the goblet so angered the Prince that he knocked it out of the hand of the tempter, leaving the two alone, locked in an intense glare.

"I will taste the poison," swore the King's Son. "For this I have come. But the hour will be mine to choose."

Finally that hour came. The Son went for one last visit with his Father. He met Him in another garden. A garden of gnarled trees and stony soil.

"Does it have to be this way?"

"It does."

"Is there no one else who can do it?"

The King swallowed. "None but you."

"Do I have to drink from the cup?"

"Yes, my Child. The same cup."

He looked at the Prince of Light. "The darkness will be great." He passed his hand over the spotless face of his Son. "The pain will be awful." Then he paused and looked at his darkened dominion. When he looked up, his eyes were moist. "But there is no other way."

The Son looked into the stars as he heard the answer. "Then, let it be done."

Slowly the words that would kill the Son began to come from the lips of the Father.

"Hour of death, moment of sacrifice, it is your moment. Rehearsed a million times on false altars with false lambs; the moment of truth has come.

"Soldiers, you think you lead him? Ropes, you think you bind him? Men, you think you sentence him? He heeds not your commands. He winces not at your lashes. It is *my* voice he obeys. It is *my* condemnation he dreads. And it is your souls he saves.

"Oh, my Son, my Child. Look up into the heavens and see my face before I turn it. Hear my voice before I silence it. Would that I could save you and them. But they don't see and they don't hear.

"The living must die so that the dying can live. The time has come to kill the Lamb.

"Here is the cup, my Son. The cup of sorrows. The cup of sin.

"Slam, mallet! Be true to your task. Let your ring be heard throughout the heavens.

"Lift him, soldiers. Lift him high to his throne of mercy. Lift him up to his perch of death. Lift him above the people that curse his name.

"Now plunge the tree into the earth. Plunge it deep into the heart of humanity. Deep into the strata of time past. Deep into the seeds of time future.

"Is there no angel to save my Isaac? Is there no hand to redeem the Redeemer?

"Here is the cup, my Son. Drink it alone."

God must have wept as he performed his task. Every lie, every lure, every act done in shadows was in that cup. Slowly, hideously they were absorbed into the body of the Son. The final act of incarnation.

The Spotless Lamb was blemished. Flames began to lick his feet.

The King obeys his own edict. "Where there is poison, there will be death. Where there are goblets, there will be fire."

The King turns away from his Prince. The undiluted wrath of a sin-hating Father falls upon his sin-filled Son. The fire envelops him. The shadow hides him. The Son looks for his Father, but his Father cannot be seen.

"My God, my God . . . why?"

The throne room is dark and cavernous. The eyes of the King are closed. He is resting.

In his dream he is again in the Garden. The cool of the evening floats across the river as the three walk. They speak of the Garden—of how it is, of how it will be.

"Father . . .", the Son begins. The King replays the word again. Father. Father. The word was a flower, petal-delicate, yet so easily crushed. Oh, how he longed for his children to call him *Father* again.

A noise snaps him from his dream. He opens his eyes and sees a transcendent figure gleaming in the doorway. "It is finished, Father. I have come home."

CHAPTER 11

COME HOME

England. Nineteenth century. Christmas. In a small town there is the tradition of a village party where all the children receive gifts. It is a festive occasion; the bright smiles of the youngsters, a tall tree at the square, colorful packages. There is a young retarded man in the town who, because of his handicap, is the victim of many cruel jokes. The trick played on him this Christmas Day is the cruelest of all.

As the mountain of gifts becomes smaller and smaller, his face grows longer and longer. He is too old for a gift, but he doesn't know that. His childlike heart is heavy as he watches everyone receive presents except himself. Then some of the boys come to him with a gift. His is the last one under the tree. His eyes dance as he looks at the brightly wrapped package. His excitement soars as he tears away the ribbons. His fingers race to rip away the paper. But as he opens the box, his heart sinks.

It's empty.

The packaging was attractive. The ribbons were colorful. The outside was enough to get him into the inside; but when he got to the inside, the box was empty![1]

Ever been there?

Many people have—

A young mother weeps silently into her pillow. All her life she had dreamed of marriage. "If only I could have a home. If only I could have a husband and a house."

So now she's married. The honeymoon has long since ended. The tunnel she dug out of one prison only led her to another. Her land of Oz has become a land of dirty diapers, car pools, and bills.

She shares a bed with a husband she doesn't love. She listens to the still sleep of a child she doesn't know how to raise. And she feels the sand of her youth slide through her fingers.

A middle-aged businessman sits in his plush office staring blankly out the window. A red German sports car awaits him in the parking lot. There is a gold ring on his finger and a gold card in his wallet. His name is in brass on a walnut door and a walnut desk. His suit is tailored. His shoes are hand-sewn, his name well known.

He should be happy. He possesses the package he set out to get when he stood at the bottom of the ladder looking up. But, now that he has what he wants, he doesn't want it. Now that he is at the top of the ladder, he sees that it is leaning against the wrong building.

He left his bride in the dust of his ambition. The kids that called him daddy don't call him daddy anymore; they have a new one. And though he has everything that success offers, he'd trade it in a heartbeat to have a home to go home to tonight.

"I've counted the holes in the ceiling tiles a hundred times." The voice shook in spite of an attempt to sound stable. "They say I'll be in this cast for six weeks. They also say I'm lucky to be alive."

His voice was barely audible through the oxygen mask. The skin on his forehead and nose was scraped.

"They keep asking me what I remember. I don't even remember getting into the car, much less driving it. I'd never tried crack before. I guess I tried too much. I'll think before I try it again. In fact, it looks like I'm going to have plenty of time for thinking."

No games. No noise. No flashing lights. Your dreams have come true but instead of letting you sleep, they are keeping you awake. What do you do at a time like this? Where do you go when the parade stops? Your failures suck the sandy foundation of your future out from under you. Now what do you do?

You can blame the world. The prodigal son could have done that. In fact, he probably did.[2]

The boy stared at his reflection in the muddy puddle. He questioned whether the face was really his. It didn't look like him.

The flame in the eyes had been extinguished. The smirk had been humbled. The devil-may-care attitude had been replaced with soberness.

He tumbled headlong and landed face first.

It wasn't enough to be friendless. It wasn't enough to be broke. It wasn't enough to pawn his ring, his coat, even his shoes. The long hours walking the streets didn't break him. You would think that the nights with only a bunkhouse pillow or the days lugging a bucket of pig-slop would force a change of heart.

But they didn't. Pride is made of stone. Hard knocks may chip it, but it takes reality's sledgehammer to break it.

His was beginning to crack.

His first few days of destitution were likely steamy with resentment. He was mad at everyone. Everyone was to blame. His friends shouldn't have bailed out on him. And his brother should come and bail him out. His boss should feed him better and his dad never should have let him go in the first place.

He named a pig after each one of them.

Failure invites finger-pointing and buck-passing. A person may be out of money, out of a job and out of friends but he is never out of people to blame.

Sometimes it's the family:

> "If my parents had taken their job more seriously . . ."
>
> "If my husband wasn't so selfish . . ."
>
> "If my kids had any respect for me . . ."
>
> "If I had been potty-trained earlier . . ."

Sometimes it's the system:

> "No one can make a good grade in this school!"
>
> "If I had been given an equal shot, I would have been promoted."
>
> "This whole place is rigged."
>
> "There is no way a person can move up in this world."

Even the church has a few bucks passed its way.

> "Oh, I'd attend church, but did you know I went to church once back in '58 and no one came to visit me?"
>
> "That group of folks? A bunch of hypocrites."
>
> "I plan on going back to church. Just as soon as I find one that is teaching the proper doctrine, housing all the homeless, feeding all the sick and giving green stamps for attendance awards, then I'll go back."

Soon you are right and everyone else is wrong. You are the victim and the world is your enemy.

A second option is to continue playing the games, only this time with a little more abandon.

My wife has a cousin named Rob. Rob is a great guy. His good heart and friendly smile endear him to everyone. He is the kind of fellow you call upon when you can't call on anyone else.

So when the Girl Scouts needed someone to dress up like the Cookie Monster at a fundraiser, who did they call? You got it. Rob.

There were a few problems. First, no one anticipated the day of the campaign would be so hot. Second, Rob didn't know that the costume would be so big. Third, who would have thought that Rob's glasses would fog up so badly that he couldn't see? As he was sitting on the stage waiting his turn to speak, the heat inside the mask covered his glasses with fog. He couldn't wipe them off—his paws were too big to fit in the eyehole.

He started to worry. Any minute he would be called upon to give a talk and he couldn't even see where the podium was!

He whispered for help. The costume was too thick and his cries went unheard.

He began to wave his hands. What he heard in response were the squeals of delight from the kids. They thought he was waving at them!

As I heard this story I chuckled . . . and then I sighed. It was too familiar. Cries for help muffled behind costumed faces? Fear hidden behind a painted smile? Signals of desperation thought to be signs of joy?

Tell me that doesn't describe our world.

Ever since Eve hemmed the fig leaves to fit Adam, we have been disguising our truths.

And we've gotten better with each generation.

Michelangelo's creativity is nothing compared to a bald man's use of a few strands of hair. Houdini would stand in awe at our capacity to squeeze lumberjack waistlines into ballerina-sized pants.

We are masters of the masquerade. Cars are driven to make a statement. Jeans are purchased to portray an image. Accents are acquired to hide a heritage. Names are dropped. Weights are lifted. Yarns are spun. Toys are purchased. Achievements are professed.

And the pain is ignored. And, with time, the real self is forgotten.

The Indians used to say that within every heart there is a knife. This knife turns like the minute hand on a clock. Every time the heart lies, the knife rotates an increment. As it turns, it cuts into the heart. As it turns, it carves a circle. The more it turns, the wider the circle becomes. After the knife has rotated one full circle, a path has been carved. The result? No more hurt, no more heart.

One option the boy in the pigpen had was to walk back into the masquerade party and pretend everything was fine. He could have carved his integrity until the pain disappeared. He could have done what millions do. He could have spent a lifetime in the pigpen pretending it was a palace. But he didn't.

Something told him that this was the moment of—and for—truth.

He looked into the water. The face he saw wasn't pretty—muddy and swollen. He looked away. "Don't think about it. You're no worse off than anybody else. Things will get better tomorrow."

The lies anticipated a receptive ear. They'd always found one before. "Not this time," he muttered. And he stared at his reflection.

"How far I have fallen." His first words of truth.

He looked into his own eyes. He thought of his father. "They always said I had your eyes." He could see the look of hurt on his father's face when he told him he was leaving.

"How I must have hurt you."

A crack zigzagged across the boy's heart.

A tear splashed into the pool. Another soon followed. Then another. Then the dam broke. He buried his face in his dirty hands as the tears did what tears do so well; they flushed out his soul.

His face was still wet as he sat near the pool. For the first time in a long time he thought of home. The memories warmed him. Memories of dinner table laughter. Memories of a warm bed. Memories of evenings on the porch with his father as they listened to hypnotic ring of the crickets.

"Father." He said the word aloud as he looked at himself. "They used to say I looked like you. Now you wouldn't even recognize me. Boy, I blew it, didn't I?"

He stood up and began to walk.

The road home was longer than he remembered. When he last traveled it, he turned heads because of his style. If he turned heads this time it was because of his stink. His clothes were torn, his hair matted, and his feet black. But that didn't bother him, because for the first time in a calendar of heartaches, he had a clean conscience.

He was going home. He was going home a changed man. Not demanding that he get what he deserved, but willing to take whatever he could get. "Give me" had been replaced with "help me," and his defiance had been replaced with repentance.

He came asking for everything with nothing to give in return. He had no money. He had no excuses.

And he had no idea how much his father had missed him.

He had no idea the number of times his father had paused between chores to look out the front gate for his son. The boy had no idea the number of times his father had awakened from restless sleep, gone into the son's room, and sat on the boy's bed. And the son would have never believed the hours the father had sat on the porch next to the empty rocking chair, looking, longing to see that familiar figure, that stride, that face.

As the boy came around the bend that led up to his house, he rehearsed his speech one more time.

"Father, I have sinned against heaven and against you."

He approached the gate and placed his hand on the latch. He began to lift it, then he paused. His plan to go home suddenly seemed silly. "What's the use?" he heard himself asking himself. "What chance do I have?" He ducked, turned around, and began to walk away.

Then he heard the footsteps. He heard the slap, slap, slap of sandals. Someone was running. He didn't turn to look. *It's probably a servant coming to chase me away or my big brother wanting to know what I'm doing back home.* He began to leave.

But the voice he heard was not the voice of a servant nor the voice of his brother; it was the voice of his father.

"Son!"

"Father?"

He turned to open the gate, but the father already had. The son looked at his father standing at the entrance. Tears glistened on his cheeks as arms stretched from east to west inviting the son to come home.

"Father, I have sinned." The words were muffled as the boy buried his face in his father's shoulder.

The two wept. For a forever they stood at the gate intertwined as one. Words were unnecessary. Repentance had been made, forgiveness had been given.

The boy was home.

If there is a scene in this story that deserves to be framed, it's the one of the father's outstretched hands. His tears are moving. His smile is stirring. But his hands call us home. Imagine those hands. Strong fingers. Palms wrinkled with lifelines. Stretching open like a wide gate, leaving entrance as the only option.

When Jesus told this parable of the loving father, I wonder, did he use his hands? When he got to this point in the story, did he open his arms to illustrate the point?

Did he perceive the thoughts of those in the audience who were thinking, "I could never go home. Not after my life."? Did he see a housewife look at the ground and a businessman shake his head as if to say, "I can't start over. I've made too big a mess."? And did he open his arms even wider as if to say, "Yes. Yes, you can. You can come home."?

Whether he did that day or not, I don't know. But I know that he did later. He later stretched his hands as open as he could. He forced his arms so wide apart that it hurt. And to prove that those arms would never fold and those hands would never close, he had them nailed open.

They still are.

1. This story is popularly attributed to Harry Emerson Fosdick.   2. Luke 15:11-27

THE FISH
AND
THE FALLS

THE JOURNEY

Once upon a distant time, when time was not and rivers had no names, there was a fish.

Born in the cascading bubbles of a rocky mountain stream, this freckled fish learned early the passion of play. He was at home in the water. He raced back and forth in the harbor made by a fallen log. He dared, on occasion, to cross the rapids by darting from rock to rock.

Each morning he witnessed the sun lift the shadowy curtain of night. It was his daily invitation to dance in the clean waters. Then, as the sun climbed higher, its warmth would lull him to slowness, giving him time to stare through the waters at the tall trees that waved and the furred visitors whose tongues would drink and then disappear.

But if the day was his time to play, the night was his time to think. This young trout, not content to know so little, kept eyes open while others closed theirs. *What is the source of this stream? Where does it go? Why is it here? Why am I here?* He pondered the questions that others never asked. And he listened at length for the answers.

Then one night he heard the roar.

The night was so bright that the moon saw herself in the stream. The fish, awake with his thoughts, recognized for the first time a noise he'd always heard.

A roar. It rumbled under the river. It vibrated the water. Suddenly the fish knew why the water was always moving.

Who is the maker of this sound? Who is the giver of this noise?

He had to know.

He swam all night without stopping, nourished by his need to know. The roar grew louder. Its thunder both frightened and compelled him.

He swam until the stars turned pale and the gray pebbles regained their colors. When he could swim no more, weariness overcame curiosity, and he stopped. He slept.

THE ENCOUNTER

The sun was warm on the trout's back. In his sleep, he dreamt he was playing again. Dashing between the rocks daring the water to catch him. He dreamt he was at home.

Then he awoke, remembering his pilgrimage.

He heard the roar. It sounded near. He opened his eyes and there it was. A wall of white foam. Water tumbling, then falling, then flying, then crashing.

It was like nothing he'd ever seen.

I will climb it and see it.

He swam to where the water crashed into the river. He attempted to swim upwards. He would ascend the falls by brute force. But the onrush of the water was too strong. Undaunted, he swam until he could swim no more, then he slept.

The next day he attempted to jump to the top. He plunged downward, deep below the churning foam. He swam deep. He swam until the water was still and dark and the roar was distant. Then he turned upward.

His fins fought from one side to the other, pushing and propelling the trout until he was swimming faster than he'd ever swam. He swam straight for the surface. Higher and higher, faster and faster. He raced through the calm waters toward the surface. He broke through the top of the water and soared high into the air. He soared so high he was sure he would land on the top of the waterfall. But he didn't. He barely rose above the foam. Then he fell.

I'll try again. Down he swam. Up he pushed. Out he flew. And down he tumbled.

He tried again. And again. And again. Ever trying to reach the top of the wall. Ever failing at his quest.

Finally night fell and the moon stood vigil over the weary young trout.

He awoke with renewed strength and a new plan. He found a safe pool off to the side of the base of the waterfall. Through the still waters he looked up. He would swim against the gentle trickle of the water as it poured over the rocks. Pleased with his wisdom, he set out. Doggedly he pushed his body to do what it wasn't made to do.

For an entire passing of the sun through the sky he struggled. He pushed on—climbing, falling; climbing, falling; climbing, falling. At one point, when his muscles begged for relief, he actually reached a ledge from which he could look out over the water below. Swollen with his achievement, he leaned too far out and tumbled headfirst into the calm pool from which he began.

Wearied from his failure, he slept.

He dreamt of the roar. He dreamt of the glory of leaving the mountain stream and dwelling in the waterfall. But when he awoke, he was still at the bottom.

When he awoke the moon was still high. It discouraged him to realize that his dream was not reality. He wondered if it was worth it. He wondered if those who never sought to know were happier.

He considered returning. The current would carry him home.

I've lived with the roar all my life and never heard it. I could simply not hear it again.

But how do you not hear the yearning of your heart? How do you turn away from discovery? How can you be satisfied with existence once you've lived with purpose?

The fish wanted nothing more than to ascend the water. But he was out of choices. He didn't know what to do. He screamed at the waterfall. "Why are you so harsh? Why are you so resistant? Why won't you help me? Don't you see I can't do it on my own? I need you!''

Just then the roar of the water began to subside. The foaming slowed. The fish looked around. The water was growing still!

Then, he felt the current again. He felt the familiar push of the rushing water. Only this time the push was from behind. The water gained momentum, slowly at first, then faster and faster until the fish found himself being carried to the tall stone wall over which had flowed the water. The wall was bare and big.

For a moment he feared that he would be slammed into it. But just as he reached the rocks, a wave formed beneath him. The trout was lifted upwards. Up he went out of the water on the tip of a rising tongue. The wave elevated him up the wall.

By now the forest was silent. The animals stood still as if they witnessed majesty. The wind ceased its stirring. The moon tilted ever so slightly in an effort to not miss the miracle.

All of nature watched as the fish rode the wave of grace. All of nature rejoiced when he reached the top. The stars raced through the blackness. The moon tilted backwards and rocked in sweet satisfaction. Bears danced. Birds hugged. The wind whistled. And the leaves applauded.

The fish was where he had longed to be. He was in the presence of the roar. What he couldn't do, the river had done. He knew immediately he would spend forever relishing the mystery.

THE ELEVENTH HOUR GIFT

Nicodemus came in the middle of the night. The centurion came in the middle of the day. The leper and the sinful woman appeared in the middle of crowds. Zacchaeus appeared in the middle of a tree. Matthew had a party for him.

The educated. The powerful. The rejected. The sick. The lonely. The wealthy. Who would have ever assembled such a crew? All they had in common were their empty hope chests, long left vacant by charlatans and profiteers. Though they had nothing to offer, they asked for everything: a new birth, a second chance, a fresh start, a clean conscience. And without exception their requests were honored.

And now, one more beggar comes with a request. Only minutes from the death of them both, he stands before the King. He will ask for crumbs. And he, like the others, will receive a whole loaf.

Skull's hill—windswept and stony. The thief—gaunt and pale.

Hinges squeak as the door of death closes on his life.

His situation is pitiful. He's taking the last step down the spiral staircase of failure. One crime after another. One rejection after another. Lower and lower he descended until he reached the bottom—a crossbeam and three spikes.

He can't hide who he is. His only clothing is the cloak of his disgrace. No fancy jargon. No impressive resumé. No Sunday school awards. Just a naked history of failure.

He sees Jesus.

Earlier he had mocked the man. When the crowd first chorused its criticism, he'd sung his part.[1] But now he doesn't mock Jesus. He studies him. He begins to wonder who this man might be.

How strange. He doesn't resist the nails, he almost invites them.

He hears the jests and the insults and sees the man remain quiet. He sees the fresh blood on Jesus' cheeks, the crown of thorns scraping Jesus' scalp and he hears the hoarse whisper, "Father, forgive them."

Why do they want him dead?

Slowly the thief's curiosity offsets the pain in his body. He momentarily forgets the nails rubbing against the raw bones of his wrists and the cramps in his calves.

He begins to feel a peculiar warmth in his heart: he begins to care; he begins to care about this peaceful martyr.

There's no anger in his eyes, only tears.

He looks at the huddle of soldiers throwing dice in the dirt, gambling for a ragged robe. He sees the sign above Jesus' head. It's painted with sarcasm: King of the Jews.

They mock him as a king. If he were crazy, they would ignore him. If he had no followers, they'd turn him away. If he was nothing to fear, they wouldn't kill him. You only kill a king if he has a kingdom.

Could it be. . . .

His cracked lips open to speak.

Then, all of a sudden, his thoughts are exploded by the accusations of the criminal on the other cross. He, too, has been studying Jesus, but studying through the blurred lens of cynicism.

"So you're the Messiah, are you? Prove it by saving yourself—and us, too, while you're at it!"[2]

It's an inexplicable dilemma—how two people can hear the same words and see the same Savior, and one see hope and the other see nothing but himself.

It was all the first criminal could take. Perhaps the crook who hurled the barb expected the other crook to take the cue and hurl a few of his own. But he didn't. No second verse was sung. What the bitter-tongued criminal did hear were words of defense.

"Don't you fear God?"

Only minutes before these same lips had cursed Jesus. Now they are defending him. Every head on the hill lifts to look at this one who spoke on behalf of the Christ. Every angel weeps and every demon gapes.

Who could have imagined this thief thinking of anyone but himself? He'd always been the bully, the purse-snatching brat. Who could remember the last time he'd come to someone's aid? But as the last grains of sand trickle through his hourglass, he performs man's noblest act. He speaks on God's behalf.

Where are those we would expect to defend Jesus?

A much more spiritual Peter has abandoned him.

A much more educated Pilate has washed his hands of him.

A much more loyal mob of countrymen has demanded his death.

A much more faithful band of disciples has scattered.

When it seems that everyone has turned away, a crook places himself between Jesus and the accusers and speaks on his behalf.

"Don't you even fear God when you are dying? We deserve to die for our evil deeds, but this man hasn't done one thing wrong."[3]

The soldiers look up. The priests cease chattering. Mary wipes her tears and raises her eyes. No one had even noticed the fellow, but now everyone looks at him.

Perhaps even Jesus looks at him. Perhaps he turns to see the one who had spoken when all others had remained silent. Perhaps he fights to focus his eyes on the one who offered this final gesture of love he'd receive while alive. I wonder, did he smile as this sheep straggled into the fold?

For that, in effect, is exactly what the criminal is doing. He is stumbling to safety just as the gate is closing. Lodged in the thief's statement are the two facts that anyone needs to recognize in order to come to Jesus. Look at the phrase again. Do you see them?

"We are getting what we deserve. This man has done nothing wrong."[4]

We are guilty and he is innocent.

We are filthy and he is pure.

We are wrong and he is right.

He is not on that cross for his sins. He is there for ours.

And once the crook understands this, his request seems only natural. As he looks into the eyes of his last hope, he made the same request any Christian has made.

"Remember me when you come into your Kingdom."[5]

No stained-glass homilies. No excuses. Just a desperate plea for help.

At this point Jesus performs the greatest miracle of the cross. Greater than the earthquake. Greater than the tearing of the temple curtain. Greater than the darkness. Greater than the resurrected saints appearing on the streets.

He performs the miracle of forgiveness. A sin-soaked criminal is received by a blood-stained Savior.

"Today you will be with me in Paradise. This is a solemn promise."[6]

Wow. Only seconds before the thief was a beggar nervously squeezing his hat at the castle door, wondering if the King might spare a few crumbs. Suddenly he's holding the whole pantry.

Such is the definition of grace.

1. Matthew 27:44   2. Luke 23:39, Living Bible   3. Luke 23:40, Living Bible   4. Luke 23:41   5. Luke 23:42 6. Luke 23:43, Living Bible

MY
DEATH
IS NOT
FINAL

CHAPTER 14

GOD
VS.
DEATH

*"I will tell you something that has
been secret: that we are not all going to die,
but we shall all be changed."*[1]

I was only going to be in Washington, D.C. for one day and that day was full. Still, I had to see it. I had read about it, heard about it, seen news reports and pictures of it, but I had to see it for myself.

"You'll only have about ten minutes," my host explained.

"Ten minutes is all I need," I told him.

So he pulled the car over and let me out.

A gray sky was shedding a coat of drizzle. I pulled my overcoat tighter around my neck. The barren trees and dead grass cast an appropriate backdrop for my mission. I walked a few hundred yards, descended a sloping sidewalk and there it was. The

Washington Monument to my left, the Lincoln Memorial to my back, and before me stretched the Vietnam Veterans Memorial.

The wailing wall of a generation. Black marble tablets carved with names that read like the roster of a high school football team more than a list of dead soldiers—Walter Faith, Richard Sala, Michael Andrews, Roy Burris, Emmet Stanton.

Each name a young life. Behind each name was a bereaved widow . . . an anguished mother . . . a fatherless child.

I looked down at my feet. There lay a dozen roses, soggy and frosty from the weather. It was the day after Valentine's Day. A girlfriend or wife had come to say, "I still remember. I haven't forgotten."

Next to me stood a trio. By the emotion on their faces, it was obvious they hadn't come out of curiosity. They had come out of grief. The one in the center caught my attention. He wore a green army coat. He was big. He was black. He was bearded. Angry tears steamed down his face. Twenty years of emotion still trying to find an exit.

A couple walked behind me. They were looking for a name. In their hands was a program that told them on what tablet to look. "Did you find it?" I heard the woman ask. "Every name has a number."

True, I thought. *Every name does have a number and sooner or later every number is called.*

It was then that I stopped looking at the names and stared at the monument. I relaxed my focus from the lettering and looked at the tablet. What I saw was sobering. I saw myself. I saw my own reflection. My face looked at me from the shiny marble. It reminded me that I, too, have been dying as long as I have been living. I, too, will someday have my name carved in a granite stone. Someday I, too, will face death.

Death. The bully on the block of life. He catches you in the alley. He taunts you in the playground. He badgers you on the way home: "You, too, will die someday."

You see him as he escorts the procession of hearse-led cars. He's in the waiting room as you walk out of the double doors of the intensive care unit. He's near as you stare at the pictures of the bloated bellies of the starving in Zimbabwe. And he'll be watching your expression as you slow your car past the crunched metal and the blanketed bodies on the highway.

"Your time is coming," he jabs.

Oh, we try to prove him wrong. We jog. We diet. We pump iron. We play golf. We try to escape it, knowing all along that we will only, at best, postpone it.

"Everyone has a number," he reminds.

And every number will be called.

He'll make your stomach tighten. He'll leave you wide-eyed and flat-footed. He'll fence you in with fear. He'll steal the joy of your youth and the peace of your final years. And if he achieves what he sets out to do, he'll make you so afraid of dying that you never learn to live.

That is why you should never face him alone. The bully is too big for you to fight by yourself. That's why you need a big brother.

Read these words and take heart. "Since the children have flesh and blood (that's you and me), he too shared in their humanity (that's Jesus, our big brother) so that by his death he might destroy him who holds the power of death—that is, the devil—and free those who all their lives were held in slavery by their fear of death. For surely it is not angels he helps, but Abraham's descendants (that's us)."[2]

Jesus unmasked death and exposed him for who he really is—a ninety-eight-pound weakling dressed up in a Charles Atlas suit. Jesus had no patience for this impostor. He couldn't sit still while death pulled the veil over life.

In fact, if you ever want to know how to conduct yourself at a funeral, don't look to Jesus for an example. He interrupted each one he ever attended.

A lifeguard can't sit still while someone is drowning. A teacher can't resist helping when a student is confused. And Jesus couldn't watch a funeral and do nothing.

In this last section, we are going to watch Jesus when he comes face-to-face with death. We are going to see his eyes mist as he sees his brothers and sisters bruised and beaten by the bully of death. We are going to see his fists clench as he encounters his enemy. We are going to . . . well, turn the page and you'll see for yourself.

You'll see why the Christian can face the bully nose-to-nose and claim the promise that echoed in the empty tomb, "My death is not final."

1. 1 Corinthians 15:51, Jerusalem Bible   2. Hebrews 2:14-16 (parentheses, mine)

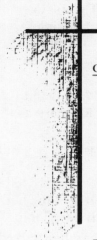

CHAPTER 15

FANTASY OR REALITY?

Two crowds. One entering the city and one leaving. They couldn't be more diverse. The group arriving buzzes with laughter and conversation. They follow Jesus. The group leaving the city is solemn—a herd of sadness hypnotized by the requiem of death. Above them rides the reason for their grief—a cold body on a wicker stretcher.

The woman at the back of the procession is the mother. She has walked this trail before. It seems like just yesterday she buried the body of her husband. Her son walked with her then. Now she walks alone, quarantined in her sadness. She is the victim of this funeral.

She is the one with no arm around her shoulder. She is the one who will sleep in the empty house tonight. She is the one who will make dinner for one and conversation with none. She is the one most

violated. The thief stole her most treasured diamond—companionship.

The followers of Jesus stop and step aside as the
procession shadows by. The blanket of mourning
muffles the laughter of the disciples. No one spoke.
What could they say? They feel the same despair felt
by the bystanders at any funeral. "Someday that will
be me."

No one intervened. What could they do? Their
only choice was to stand and stare as the mourners
shuffled past.

Jesus, however, knew what to say and what to do.
When he saw the mother, his heart began to break
. . . and his lips began to tighten. He glared at the
angel of death that hovered over the body of the boy.
"Not this time, Satan. This boy is mine."

At that moment the mother walked in front of
him. Jesus spoke to her. "Don't cry." She stopped
and looked into this stranger's face. If she wasn't
shocked by his presumption, you can bet some of the
witnesses were.

Don't cry? Don't cry? What kind of request is
that?

A request only God can make.

Jesus stepped toward the bier and touched it.
The pall-bearers stopped marching. The mourners
ceased moaning. As Jesus stared at the boy, the crowd
was silent.

The demon had been perched spider-like over
the body. He was enjoying the parade. He was the
warden. The people were the prisoners. He was
marching the condemned to execution. They were
watching from behind invisible bars, imprisoned by

their impermanence. He had relished the fear in the faces. He had giggled at their despair.

Then he heard the voice. That voice . . . he knew the owner. His back arched and he hissed instinctively.

He turned. He didn't see what others saw. He didn't see the face of a Nazarene. He didn't hear the voice of a man. He saw the wrath of God. He heard the command of a King.

"Get out of here."

He didn't have to be told twice.

Jesus turned his attention to the dead boy. "Young man," his voice was calm, "come back to life again."

The living stood motionless as the dead came to life. Wooden fingers moved. Gray-pale cheeks blushed. The dead man sat up.

Luke's description of what happened next is captivating.

"Jesus gave him back to his mother."[1]

How would you feel at a moment like this? What would you do? A stranger tells you not to weep as you look at your dead son. One who refuses to mourn in the midst of sorrow calls the devil's bluff, then shocks you with a call into the cavern of death. Suddenly what had been taken is returned. What had been stolen is retrieved. What you had given up, you are given back.

Jesus must have smiled as the two embraced. Stunned, the crowd broke into cheers and applause. They hugged each other and slapped Jesus on the back. Someone proclaimed the undeniable, "God has come to help his people."[2]

Jesus gave the woman much more than her son. He gave her a secret—a whisper that was overheard by us. "That," he said pointing at the cot, "that is fantasy. This," he grinned, putting an arm around the boy, "this is reality."

1. Luke 7:15   2. Luke 7:16

THE SPARKLE FROM ETERNITY

Wallace was an important man. He was the kind of man you would find leading a prayer at the football games or serving as president of the Lion's Club. He wore a title and a collar and had soft hands with no callouses.

He had a nice office just off the sanctuary. His secretary was a bit stale but he wasn't. He had a warm smile that melted your apprehension as you walked through his office door. He sat in a leather swivel chair and had diplomas on the wall. And he had a way of listening that made you willing to tell secrets you'd never told anyone.

He was a good man. His marriage wasn't all it could be, but it was better than most. His church was full. His name was respected. He was a fifteen-hand-icap golfer and the church bought him a member-ship at the country club to commemorate his twentieth year with the congregation. People recognized him in public and flocked to hear him on Easter and Christmas. His retirement account was growing and he was less than a decade from hanging up the frock and settling down to an autumn of soft wine and good books.

If he committed a sin, no one knew it. If he had a fear, no one heard it—which may have been his gravest sin.

Wallace loved people. This morning, though, he doesn't want people. He wants to be alone. He rings his secretary and advises her that he is not taking any more calls for the rest of the day. She doesn't think it unusual. He's been on the phone all morning. She thinks he needs time to study. She is partly correct. He has been on the phone all morning and he does need time. Not time to study, however. Time to weep.

Wallace looks at the eight-by-ten photo that sits on the mahogany credenza behind his desk. Through watery eyes he gazes at his twelve-year-old daughter. Braces. Pigtails. Freckles. She is a reflection of his wife—blue eyes, brown hair, pug nose. The only thing she got from her father was his heart. She owns that. And he has no intention of requesting that she return it.

She isn't his only child, but she is his last. And she is his only daughter. He'd built a fence of protection around his little girl. Maybe that is why the last few days had hurt so badly. The fence had crumbled.

It began six days ago. She came home early from school feverish and irritable. His wife put her to bed, thinking it was the flu. During the night the fever rose. The next morning they rushed her to the hospital.

The doctors were puzzled. They couldn't pinpoint the problem. They could only agree on one thing—she was sick and getting sicker.

Wallace had never known such helplessness. He didn't know how to handle his pain. He was so accustomed to being strong, he didn't know how to be weak. He assured all who called that his daughter was fine. He assured all who inquired that God was a great God. He assured everyone but himself.

Inside, his emotions were a mighty river. And his dam was beginning to crack. It was the call from the doctor this morning that broke it. "She is in a coma."

Wallace hangs up the phone and tells his secretary to hold the calls. He reaches over and takes the picture and holds it in his hands. Suddenly the words swirl in his head like a merry-go-round. "It's not fair, it's not fair."

He leans over, holds the picture to his face and weeps.

Nothing is right about it. Nothing. "Why a twelve-year-old girl? Why her, for mercy sakes?" His face hardens as he looks out his window toward the gray sky.

"Why don't you take me?" he screams.

He sits up. He walks over to the coffee table by the couch and picks up the box of tissues he keeps handy for counselees. As he's blowing his nose, he looks out the window into the courtyard of the church. An old man sits reading a paper. Another enters and sits beside him and throws bread crumbs on the cobbles. There's a rustle of wings as a covey of pigeons flutters off the roof and snatches up the food.

Don't you know my daughter is dying? How can you act as if nothing is wrong?

He's thinking about his daughter. In the springtime she used to come by every day on the way home from school. She would wait in the courtyard for him to walk her home. He would hear her chasing pigeons below and know it was time to go. He'd stop what he was doing, stand at this same window and watch her. He'd watch her walk a tightrope on the curb around the garden. He'd watch her pick a wildflower out of the grass. He'd watch her spin around and around until she became so dizzy that she'd fall on her back and watch the clouds spin in the sky.

"Oh, Princess," he'd say. "My little girl." Then he'd stack his books and headaches on his desk and go down to meet her.

But it is not springtime and his daughter is not in the courtyard. It is winter, his little girl is nearly dead and two old men are sitting on a bench.

"Dear, dear Princess."

Suddenly a third man enters the courtyard. He tells something to the other two. Then the three hurry out. *Must be a fight,* Wallace thinks to himself. Then he remembers. *The teacher. He is here.*

He'd almost forgotten. Jesus was arriving today. As Wallace was leaving the house this morning, his neighbor had asked him if he was going to see the controversial teacher.

Inwardly, he'd scoffed at the idea. "No, too busy today," he'd answered with a wave, knowing that even on a slow day he wouldn't take time to go see an itinerant preacher. Especially this one.

The journals from headquarters had branded this guy a maverick. Some even said he was insane. But the crowds hung around him like he was God's gift to humanity.

I'm going. Wallace replayed the neighbor's response in his head.

"Yeah," Wallace had said to himself, "You also subscribe to *National Enquirer.*"

"They say he can heal . . .," he recalled his neighbor say.

Wallace stood up straight. Then he relaxed. "Don't be foolish."

"Faith-healers are an insult to our profession," he had declared while lecturing at the seminary last fall. "Parasites of the people, charlatans of the church, prophets for profit." He'd seen these guys on television, stuffed into double-breasted suits, wearing mannequin smiles and powdered faces. He shakes his head and walks back to his desk. He picks up the photograph.

He stares at the face of the child who was about to be taken from him. "They say he can heal. . . ."

Wallace began to weigh the options. "If I go and am recognized, it will mean my job. But if she dies and he could have done something. . . ." A man reaches a point where his desperation is a notch above his dignity. He shrugs his shoulders. "What choice do I have?"

The events of that afternoon redirected Wallace's life. He told the story whenever he had a chance.

I circled the bus terminal three times before I found a place to park. The cold wind bit my ears as I fumbled through my pockets looking for parking meter change. I buttoned my overcoat up to the knot of my tie, turned into the wind and walked.

I passed a pawn shop window still flocked with Season's Greetings. Someone came out of a bar as I walked by. A dozen or so teens in skintight pants leaned against a brick wall. One flipped a cigarette butt at my feet. Three men in leather jackets and jeans warmed hands over a fire in a ten-gallon drum. One of them chuckled as I walked by. "Looky there, a poodle in the pound." I didn't turn around. If he was talking about me, I didn't want to know.

I felt awkward. It had been years since I'd been on this side of town. I glanced over at my reflection in a drugstore window. Wool overcoat. Wingtip shoes. Gray suit. Red tie. No wonder I was turning heads. Their question was written in their eyes. "What brings Mr. White-collar across the tracks?" The bus station was packed. I barely squeezed through the door.

Once I got in I couldn't have gotten out. Heads bobbed and ducked like corks on a lake. Everyone was trying to get across the room to the side where the de-boarded passengers entered the terminal. I managed to squeeze through ahead of them. They were just curious; I was desperate.

As I reached the window I saw him. He stood near the bus. He had only been able to advance a couple of strides against the wall of people.

He looked too normal. He wore a corduroy jacket, the kind with patches on the elbows. His slacks weren't new, but they were nice. No tie. His hairline receded a bit before it became a flow of brown curls. I couldn't hear his voice, but I could see his face. His eyebrows were bushy. He had a gleam in his eyes and a grin on his lips—as if he were watching you unwrap the birthday present he just gave you.

He was so different from what I had anticipated I had to ask a lady next to me if that was him.

"That's him," she smiled. "That's Jesus."

He bent over and disappeared for a minute and surfaced holding a toddler. He smiled. With hands around the little boy's chest, he pushed him high into the air and held him there. The hands were rugged and slender. Someone had told me that Jesus grew up in Mississippi—the son of a mechanic in Tupelo. He brought the little boy down and began walking toward the door.

I knew if he entered the bus station, I'd never get him out. I put my hands flat against the window pane and began edging along the window. People complained but I moved anyway.

When I got to the doorway, so did Jesus. Our eyes met. I froze. I guess I hadn't considered what I would say to him. Maybe I thought he would recognize me. Maybe I thought he'd ask me if there was anything he could do. "Oh, my daughter is sick and I thought you might say a prayer. . . ."

That's not how it came out. The words log-jammed in my throat. I felt my eyes water, my chin quiver, and my knees hit the uneven pavement. "It's my daughter, my little girl . . . she's very sick. Could you please touch her so that she won't die?"

I regretted the words as soon as I said them. *If he's a man, then I've asked the impossible. If he's more than a man, what right do I have to make such a request?*

I didn't dare look up. I was ashamed. If the crowd was going anywhere they were going to have to move around me. I didn't have the courage to raise my face.

I guess he knew I didn't. He did it for me.

I felt his fingers under my chin. He lifted my head. He didn't have to raise it far. He had knelt down in front of me. I looked into his eyes. The gaze of this young preacher embraced this old pastor like the arms of an old friend. I knew, then, that I knew this man. From somewhere I'd seen that look. I knew those eyes.

"Take me to her." His hand moved under my arm. He helped me stand. "Where is your car?"

"A car? This way!" I grabbed his hand and began to fight a path through the crowd. It wasn't easy. With my free hand I moved people like I was parting stalks of corn in a cornfield. Faces tumbled in on us. Young mothers wanting a blessing for their children. Old faces with caved-in mouths wanting release from pain.

Suddenly I lost his hand. It slipped out. I stopped and turned and saw him standing and looking. His abrupt stop surprised the crowd. They hushed. I noticed his face was pale. He spoke as if speaking to himself.

"Someone touched me."

"What?" one of his own men inquired.

"Someone touched me."

I thought he was telling a joke. He turned, slowly studying each face. For the life of me, I couldn't tell if he was angry or delighted. He was looking for someone he didn't know but knew he'd know when he saw her.

"I touched you." The voice was beside me. Jesus pivoted.

"It was me. I'm sorry." The curtain of the crowd parted leaving a girl on center stage. She was thin, almost frail. I could have wrapped my hand around her upper arm and touched my finger to my thumb. Her skin was dark and her hair was in a hundred braids with beads on each end. She was coatless. She hugged her arms to herself—hands squeezing bony elbows as much out of fear as out of cold.

"Don't be afraid." Jesus assured. "What was wrong?"

"I have AIDS."

Someone behind me gasped. Several took a step back.

Jesus stepped towards her. "Tell me about it."

She looked at him, looked around at the throng of people, swallowed and began. "I was out of money. The doctors said it was just a matter of time. I didn't have anywhere else to go. But now. . . ."

She lowered her eyes and began to smile. She smiled as if someone had just whispered some good news in her ear.

I looked back at Jesus. My lands, if he wasn't smiling too! The two stood there and stared at each other, smiling like they were the only two kids in class who knew the answer to the teacher's question.

It was then I saw the look again. The same gaze that only moments before met me as I looked up from the pavement met her. Those same eyes that I knew I'd seen I saw again. Where? Where had I seen those eyes?

I turned and looked at the girl. For a moment she looked at me. I wanted to say something to her. I think she felt the same urge. We were so different, but suddenly we had everything in common: What a strange couple we were. She with her needle-tracked arms and midnight lovers; I with my clean fingernails and sermon outlines. I had spent my life telling people not to be like her. She'd spent her life avoiding hypocrites like me. But now we were thrust together against the enemy of death, desperately hoping that this country preacher could tie a knot in the end of our frazzled ropes so we could hang on.

Jesus spoke. "It was your faith that did it. Now go and enjoy life."

She resisted all effort to hide her joy. She smiled, looked back at Jesus, and jumped up and kissed him on the cheek.

The crowd laughed, Jesus blushed, and she disappeared.

I hadn't noticed, but while Jesus was speaking some other men had worked their way into the crowd. They were standing behind me. When I heard them speak, I immediately recognized their voices. They were from my congregation.

One put his hand on my shoulder. "There's no need to bother this teacher anymore, your daughter is dead."

The words came at me like darts, but Jesus intercepted them: "Don't be afraid, just trust me."

The next few moments were a blur of activity. We raced through the crowd, jumped in the car of the man who brought the news and sped to the hospital.

The waiting room was chaotic. Church members, neighbors, and friends were already gathering. Several wept openly. My wife, seated in one of the chairs, was pale and speechless. Her eyes were red. Her hand trembled as she brushed away a tear.

As I entered, people came to comfort me. Jesus stepped in front of them. They stopped and stared at this stranger.

"Why are you crying?" he asked. "She isn't dead, she's only asleep."

They were stunned. They were insulted. "Of all the insensitive things to say," someone shouted. "Who are you anyway?"

"Get that joker out of here!"

But leaving was the last thing Jesus had on his agenda. He turned and within a few seconds was standing in front of my daughter's hospital room. He signaled for a few of us to follow. We did.

The six of us stood at my daughter's bedside. Her face was ashen. Her lips dry and still. I touched her hand. It was cold. Before I could say anything, Jesus' hand was on mine. With the exception of one instant he never took his eyes off my daughter. But during that instant, he looked at me. He looked at me with that same look, that same slight smile. He was giving another gift and couldn't wait to see the response when it was opened.

"Princess," the words were said softly, almost in a whisper," Get up!"

Her head turned slightly as if hearing a voice. Jesus stood back. Her upper body leaned forward until she was upright in bed. Her eyes opened. She turned and put her bare feet on the floor and stood.

No one moved as my wife and I watched our girl walk toward us. We held her for an eternity—half believing it couldn't be true and half not wanting to know if it wasn't. But it was.

"Better get her something to eat," Jesus teased with a smile, "she's probably famished." Then he turned to leave.

I reached out and touched his shoulder. My willingness was in my eyes. "Let me return the favor. I'll introduce you to the right people. I'll get you speaking engagements at the right places."

"Let's keep this between us, okay?" and he and three speechless friends left the room.

For weeks after that day I was puzzled. Oh, of course I was exuberant. But my joy was peppered with mystery. Everywhere I went I saw his face. His look followed me. Even as I write this, I can see it.

Head cocked just a bit. Tender twinkle of anticipation under bushy brows. That look that whispered, "Come here, I've got a secret."

And now I know where I'd seen it before. In fact I've seen it again—several times.

I saw it in the eyes of the cancer patient I visited yesterday. Bald from chemotherapy. Shadowed eyes from the disease. Her skin was soft and her hand bony. She recognized me when she awoke. She didn't even say hello. She just lofted her eyebrows, sparkled that sparkle and said, "I'm ready, Wallace. I'm ready to go."

I saw it last week as I spoke at a funeral. The widower, a wrinkled-faced man with white hair and bifocals. He didn't weep like the others. In fact, at one point I think I saw him smile. I shook his hand afterwards. "Don't worry about me," he exclaimed. Then he motioned for me to lean down so he could say something in my ear. "I know where she is."

But it was this morning that I saw it the clearest. I'd wanted to ask her for days, but the right moment never came. This morning it did. At the breakfast table, just the two of us, she with her cereal, I with my paper, I turned to my daughter and asked her. "Princess?"

"Uh huh?"

"What was it like?"

"What?"

"While you were gone. What was it like?"

She didn't say anything. She just turned her head slightly and looked out the window. When she turned around again, the sparkle was there. She opened her mouth and then closed it, then opened it again. "It's a secret, Dad. A secret too good for words."

Peace where there should be pain. Confidence in the midst of crisis. Hope defying despair. That's what that look says. It is a look that knows the answer to the question asked by every mortal, "Does death have the last word?" I can see Jesus wink as he gives the answer. "Not on your life."

(Based on Mark 5:22-43; Matthew 9:18-26 and Luke 8:41-56)

ROUND THREE: "LAZARUS, COME OUT!"

When the famous agnostic Robert Ingersoll died, the printed funeral program left this solemn instruction, "There will be no singing."

Few feel like singing in the face of death. Running, perhaps. Crying, probably. But singing? Not at death. Death steals our reason to sing. Death takes the songs from our lips and leaves in their place stilled tongues and tear-flooded cheeks.

There was no singing at the funeral Jesus attended either. Mourning. Weeping. Wailing. But no singing.

The house was more like a prison than a residence. People shuffled about aimlessly, their faces pasty-white and their eyes full moons of fear. On their lips was no music, no laughter—only the foreboding news that reminded them of their own fate: Another prisoner had been marched from death row to the gallows. Lazarus was dead. They were in prison awaiting their turn.

Shoikoi Yokoi spent twenty-eight years in a prison. Not a prison of walls, but a prison of fear. When the tide began to turn in World War II, Shokoi was a Japanese soldier on the island of Guam. Fearing that defeat meant certain capture by American forces, he ran into the jungle and hid in a cave. He later learned the war was over by reading one of the thousands of leaflets that were dropped into the jungle by American planes. Still, he feared being taken as prisoner, so he remained in his cave.

For the over a quarter of a century he came out only at night. He existed on frogs, rats, roaches and mangoes. It was only when some hunters discovered him that he was convinced that it was safe to leave the jungle.

"Shocking," we say. "How could a man be so blind?"

"Tragic," we sigh. "What a waste of life."

"A pity," we lament, "that a human would be so imprisoned by fear that he would cease to live."

A life wasted pacing up and down in a self-made cell of fear. It *is* shocking. It *is* tragic. It *is* a pity. And it is also very common.

The fear of death has filled a thousand prisons. You can't see the walls. You can't see the warden. You can't see the locks. But you can see the prisoners. You can see them as they sit on their bunks and bemoan their fate. They want to live, but they can't because they are doomed to do what they most want to avoid—they will die.

And, oh how restrictive is the ball and chain of death. You try to run away from it—you can't. You try to run with it—it is too heavy. You try to ignore it, and it yanks you into reality.

Just yesterday I visited a home that was wearing the black wreath of death. The youngest of three daughters, a recently married twenty-two-year-old, had been killed in a collision between an eighteen-wheeler and a bus. The eyes that met me at the door were those of a prisoner. The family was held hostage by the answerless questions. Taken captive by sadness, they couldn't take a dozen steps without walking into a brick wall of disbelief.

It was enough to make you cry. It is enough to make God cry.

Jesus' throat tightened as he walked among the inmates. He gazed at the chalky faces through watery eyes. How long would they listen to Satan's lie? How long would they be in bondage? What would he have to do to convince them? Hadn't he proven it at Nain? Was the raising of Jairus's daughter not proof enough? How long would these people lock themselves into this man-made prison of fear? He had shown them they key to unlock their door. Why didn't they use it?

"Show me the tomb."

They led him to the burial place of Lazarus. It was a cave with a stone laid across the entrance. Over the stone was spun the spiderweb of finality. "No more!" the stone boasted. "No more shall these hands move. No longer shall this tongue speak. No more!"

Jesus wept. He wept not for the dead but for the living. He wept not for the one in the cave of death but for those in the cave of fear. He wept for those who, though alive, were dead. He wept for those who, though free, were prisoners, held captive by their fear of death.

"Move the stone." The command was soft but firm.

"But, Jesus, it will . . . it will stink."

"Move the stone so you will see God."

Stones have never stood in God's way. They didn't in Bethany two thousand years ago. And they didn't in Europe a hundred years ago.

She was a Hanoverian countess. If she was known for anything, she was known for her disbelief in God and her conviction that no one could call life from a tomb.

Before her death, she left specific instructions that her tomb was to be sealed with a slab of granite; she asked that blocks of stone be placed around her tomb and that the corners of the blocks be fastened together and to the granite slab by heavy iron clamps.

This inscription was placed on the granite rock:

This burial place,
purchased to all eternity,
must never be opened.

All that any man could do to seal the tomb was done. The countess had insured that her tomb would serve as a mockery to the belief in the resurrection. A small birch tree, however, had other plans. Its root found its way between the slabs and grew deep into the ground. Over the years it forced its way until the iron clamps popped loose and the granite lid was raised. The stone cover is now resting against the trunk of the birch, the boastful epitaph permanently silenced by the work of a determined tree . . . or a powerful God.

"Lazarus, come out!"

It took only one call. Lazarus heard his name. His eyes opened beneath the wrap. The cloth-covered hands raised. Knees lifted, feet touched the ground, and the dead man came out.

"Take the grave clothes off of him and let him go."

There is a story told in Brazil about a missionary who discovered a tribe of Indians in a remote part of the jungle. They lived near a large river. The tribe was friendly and in need of medical attention. A contagious disease was ravaging the population and people were dying daily. An infirmary was located in another part of the jungle and the missionary determined that the only hope for the tribe was to go to the hospital for treatment and inoculations. In order to reach the hospital, however, the Indians would have to cross the river—a feat they were unwilling to perform.

The river, they believed, was inhabited by evil spirits. To enter the water meant certain death. The missionary set about the difficult task of overcoming the superstition of the tribe.

He explained how he had crossed the river and arrived unharmed. No luck. He led the people to the bank and placed his hand in the water. The people still wouldn't believe him. He walked out into the river and splashed water on his face. The people watched closely, yet were still hesitant. Finally he turned and dove into the water. He swam beneath the surface until he emerged on the other side.

Having proven that the power of the river was a farce, the missionary punched a triumphant fist into the air. He had entered the water and escaped. The Indians broke into cheers and followed him across.

Jesus saw people enslaved by their fear of a cheap power. He explained that the river of death was nothing to fear. The people wouldn't believe him. He touched a boy and called him back to life. The followers were still unconvinced. He whispered life into the dead body of a girl. The people were still cynical. He let a dead man spend four days in a grave and then called him out. Is that enough? Apparently not. For it was necessary for him to enter the river, to submerge himself in the water of death before people would believe that death had been conquered.

But after he did, after he came out on the other side of death's river, it was time to sing . . . it was time to celebrate.

1. John 11:1-37

THE CELEBRATION

A party was the last thing Mary expected as she approached the tomb on that Sunday morning. The last few days had brought nothing to celebrate. The Jews could celebrate—Jesus was out of the way. The soldiers could celebrate—their work was done. But Mary couldn't celebrate. To her the last few days had brought nothing but tragedy.

Mary had been there. She had heard the leaders clamor for Jesus' blood. She had witnessed the Roman whip rip the skin off his back. She had winced as the thorns sliced his brow and wept at the weight of the cross.

In the Louvre there is a painting of the scene of the cross. In the painting the stars are dead and the world is wrapped in darkness. In the shadows there is a kneeling form. It is Mary. She is holding her hands and lips against the bleeding feet of the Christ.

We don't know if Mary did that, but we know she could have. She was there. She was there to hold her arm around the shoulder of Mary the mother of Jesus. She was there to close his eyes. She was there.

So it's not surprising that she wants to be there again.

In the early morning mist she arises from her mat, takes her spices and aloes and leaves her house, past the Gate of Gennath and up to the hillside. She anticipates a somber task. By now the body will be swollen. His face will be white. Death's odor will be pungent.

A gray sky gives way to gold as she walks up the narrow trail. As she rounds the final bend, she gasps. The rock in front of the grave is pushed back.

"Someone took the body." She runs to awaken Peter and John. They rush to see for themselves. She tries to keep up with them but can't.

Peter comes out of the tomb bewildered and John comes out believing, but Mary just sits in front of it weeping. The two men go home and leave her alone with her grief.

But something tells her she is not alone. Maybe she hears a noise. Maybe she hears a whisper. Or maybe she just hears her own heart tell her to take a look for herself.

Whatever the reason, she does. She stoops down, sticks her head into the hewn entrance and waits for her eyes to adjust to the dark.

"Why are you crying?" She sees what looks to be a man, but he's white—radiantly white. He is one of two lights on either end of the vacant slab. Two candles blazing on an altar.

"Why are you crying?" An uncommon question to be asked in a cemetery. In fact, the question is rude. That is, unless the questioner knows something the questionee doesn't.

"They have taken my Lord away, and I don't know where they have put him."

She still calls him "my Lord." As far as she knows his lips were silent. As far as she knows, his corpse had been carted off by grave robbers. But in spite of it all, he is still her Lord.

Such devotion moves Jesus. It moves him closer to her. So close, she hears him breathing. She turns and there he stands. She thinks he is the gardener.

Now, Jesus could have revealed himself at this point. He could have called for an angel to present him or a band to announce his presence. But he didn't.

"Why are you crying? Who is it you are looking for?"[1]

He doesn't leave her wondering long, just long enough to remind us that he loves to surprise us. He waits for us to despair of human strength and then intervenes with heavenly. God waits for us to give up and then—surprise!

Has it been a while since you let God surprise you? It's easy to reach the point where we have God figured out.

We know exactly what God does. We break the code. We chart his tendencies. God is a computer. If we push all the right buttons and insert the right data, God is exactly who we thought he was. No variations. No alterations. God is a jukebox. Insert a tithe. Punch in the right numbers and—bam—the divine music we want fills the room.

I look across my desk and see a box of tissues. Ten minutes ago that box sat in the lap of a young woman—mid-thirties, mother of three. She told me of the telephone call she received from her husband this morning. He wants a divorce. She had to leave work and weep. She wanted a word of hope.

I reminded her that God is at his best when our life is at its worst. God has been known to plan a celebration in a cemetery. I told her, "Get ready, you may be in for a surprise."

Have you got God figured out? Have you got God captured on a flowchart and frozen on a flannel board? If so, then listen. Listen to God's surprises.

Hear the rocks meant for the body of the adulterous woman drop to the ground.

Listen as Jesus invites a death row convict to ride with him to the kingdom in the front seat of the limo.

Listen as the Messiah whispers to the Samaritan woman, "I who speak to you am he."

Listen to the widow from Nain eating dinner with her son who is supposed to be dead.

And listen to the surprise as Mary's name is spoken by a man she loved—a man she had buried.

"Miriam."

God appearing at the strangest of places. Doing the strangest of things. Stretching smiles where there had hung only frowns. Placing twinkles where there were only tears. Hanging a bright star in a dark sky. Arching rainbows in the midst of thunder clouds. Calling names in a cemetery.

"Miriam," he said softly, "surprise!"

Mary was shocked. It's not often you hear your name spoken by an eternal tongue. But when she did, she recognized it. And when she did, she responded correctly. She worshiped him.

The scene has all the elements of a surprise party—secrecy, wide eyes, amazement, gratitude. But this celebration is timid in comparison with the one that is being planned for the future. It will be similar to Mary's, but a lot bigger. Many more graves will open. Many more names will be called. Many more knees will bow. And many more seekers will celebrate.

It's going to be some party. I plan to make sure my name is on the guest list. How about you?

"No eye has seen,
no ear has heard,
no mind has conceived
what God has prepared for those who love him."[2]

1. John 20:1-18   2. 1 Corinthians 2:9

THE FINAL GLANCE

"Max, your dad's awake."

I had been watching a movie on television. One of those thrillers that takes you from the here and now and transports you to the somewhere and sometime. My mother's statement seemed to come from another world. The real world.

I turned toward my father. He was looking at me.

His head was all he could turn. Lou Gehrig's disease had leeched his movement, taking from him everything but his faith . . . and his eyes.

It was his eyes that called me to walk over to his bedside. I had been home for almost two weeks, on special leave from Brazil, due to his worsening condition. He had slept most of the last few days, awakening only when my mother would bathe him or clean his sheets.

Next to his bed was a respirator—a metronome of mortality that pushed air into his lungs through a hole in his throat. The bones in his hand protruded like spokes in an umbrella. His fingers, once firm and strong, were curled and lifeless. I sat on the edge of his bed and ran my hands over his barreled rib cage. I put my hand on his forehead. It was hot . . . hot and damp. I stroked his hair.

"What is it, Dad?"

He wanted to say something. His eyes yearned. His eyes refused to release me. If I looked away for a moment, they followed me, and were still looking when I looked back.

"What is it?"

I'd seen that expression before. I was seven years old, eight at the most. Standing on the edge of a diving board for the first time, wondering if I would survive the plunge. The board dipped under my seventy pounds. I looked behind me at the kids who were pestering me to hurry up and jump. I wondered what they would do if I asked them to move over so I could get down. Tar and feather me, I supposed.

So caught between ridicule and a jump into certain death, I did the only thing I knew to do—I shivered.

Then I heard him, "It's all right, son, come on in." I looked down. My father had dived in. He was treading water awaiting my jump. Even as I write, I can see his expression—tanned face, wet hair, broad smile, and bright eyes. His eyes were assuring and earnest. Had he not said a word, they would have conveyed the message. But he did speak. "Jump, it's all right."

So I jumped.

Twenty-three years later the tan was gone, the hair thin and the face drawn. But the eyes hadn't changed. They were bold. And their message hadn't changed. I knew what he was saying. Somehow he knew I was afraid. Somehow he perceived that I was shivering as I looked into the deep. And somehow, he, the dying, had the strength to comfort me, the living.

I placed my cheek in the hollow of his. My tears dripped on his hot face. I said softly what his throat wanted to, but couldn't. "It's all right," I whispered. "It's going to be all right."

When I raised my head, his eyes were closed. I would never see them open again.

He left me with a final look. One last statement of the eyes. One farewell message from the captain before the boat would turn out to sea. One concluding assurance from a father to a son, "It's all right."

Perhaps it was a similar look that stirred the soul of the soldier during those six hours one Friday.

He was uneasy. He had been since noon.

It wasn't the deaths that troubled him. The centurion was no stranger to finality. Over the years he'd grown calloused to the screams of the crucified. He'd mastered the art of numbing his heart. But this crucifixion plagued him.

The day began as had a hundred others—dreadfully. It was bad enough to be in Judea, but it was hell to spend hot afternoons on a rocky hill supervising the death of pickpockets and rabble-rousers. Half the crowd taunted, half cried. The soldiers griped. The priests bossed. It was a thankless job in a strange land. He was ready for the day to be over before it began.

He was curious at the attention given to the flat-footed peasant. He smiled as he read the sign that would go on the cross. The condemned looked like anything but a king. His face was lumpy and bruised. His back arched slightly and his eyes faced downward. "Some harmless hick," mused the centurion. "What could he have done?"

Then Jesus raised his head. He wasn't angry. He wasn't uneasy. His eyes were strangely calm as they stared from behind the bloody mask. He looked at those who knew him—moving deliberately from face to face as if he had a word for each.

For just a moment he looked at the centurion—for a second, the Roman looked into the purest eyes he'd ever seen. He didn't know what the look meant. But the look made him swallow and his stomach feel empty. As he watched the soldier grab the Nazarene and yank him to the ground, something told him this was not going to be a normal day.

As the hours wore on, the centurion found himself looking more and more at the one on the center cross. He didn't know what to do with the Nazarene's silence. He didn't know what to do with his kindness.

But most of all, he was perplexed by the darkness. He didn't know what to do with the black sky in mid-afternoon. No one could explain it . . . no one even tried. One minute the sun—the next the darkness. One minute the heat, the next a chilly breeze. Even the priests were silenced.

For a long while the centurion sat on a rock and stared at the three silhouetted figures. Their heads were limp, occasionally rolling from side to side. The jeering was silent . . . eerily silent. Those who had wept, now waited.

Suddenly the center head ceased to bob. It yanked itself erect. Its eyes opened in a flash of white. A roar sliced the silence. "It is finished."[1] It wasn't a yell. It wasn't a scream. It was a roar . . . a lion's roar. From what world that roar came the centurion didn't know, but he knew it wasn't this one.

The centurion stood up from the rock and took a few paces toward the Nazarene. As he got closer he could tell that Jesus was staring into the sky. There was something in his eyes that the soldier had to see. But after only a few steps, he fell. He stood and fell again. The ground was shaking, gently at first and now violently. He tried once more to walk and was able to take a few steps and then fall . . . at the foot of the cross.

He looked up into the face of this one near death. The King looked down at the crusty old centurion. Jesus' hands were fastened—they couldn't reach out. His feet were nailed to timber, they couldn't walk toward him. His head was heavy with pain, he could scarcely move it. But his eyes . . . they were afire.

They were unquenchable. They were the eyes of God.

Perhaps that is what made the centurion say what he said. He saw the eyes of God. He saw the same eyes that had been seen by a near-naked adulteress in Jerusalem, a friendless divorcee in Samaria, and a four-day-dead Lazarus in a cemetery. The same eyes that didn't close upon seeing man's futility, didn't turn away at man's failure, and didn't wince upon witnessing man's death.

"It's all right," God's eyes said, "I've seen the storms and it's still all right."

The centurion's convictions began to flow together like rivers. "This was no carpenter," he spoke under his breath. "This was no peasant. This was no normal man."

He stood and looked around at the rocks that had fallen and the sky that had blackened. He turned and stared at the soldiers as they stared at Jesus with frozen faces. He turned and watched as the eyes of Jesus lifted and looked toward home. He listened as the parched lips parted and the swollen tongue spoke for the last time.

"Father, into your hands I entrust my spirit."[2]

Had the centurion not said it, the soldiers would have. Had the centurion not said it, the rocks would have—as would have the angels, the stars, even the demons. But he did say it. It fell to a nameless foreigner to state what they all knew.

"Surely this man was the Son of God."[3]

Six hours on one Friday. Six hours that jut up on the plain of human history like Mount Everest in a desert. Six hours that have been deciphered, dissected, and debated for two thousand years.

What do these six hours signify? They claim to be the door in time through which eternity entered man's darkest caverns. They mark the moments that the Navigator descended into the deepest waters to leave anchor points for his followers.

What does that Friday mean?

For the life blackened with failure, that Friday means forgiveness.

For the heart scarred with futility, that Friday means purpose.

And for the soul looking into this side of the tunnel of death, that Friday means deliverance.

Six hours. One Friday.

What do *you* do with those six hours on that Friday?

ANCHORING DEEP

A MESSAGE FROM MAX

Do you know many people who have intentionally turned their backs on God and stomped away in anger? Neither do I. Do you know many people who gradually lost their faith over an extended period of time? So do I.

Few abandon the faith out of anger at God or disbelief in the Scriptures. If you vacate your church pew you probably won't do so overnight. It will be a subtle, casual abandonment. Read these words from Hebrews and see how one writer describes the process:

"We must pay more careful attention, therefore, to what we have heard, so that we do not drift away" (Hebrews 2:1).

What is the danger that faces any person attempting to stay spiritually afloat? Drifting. Getting off course. Aimlessly floating. A directionless meander that leaves you in uncharted and unfamiliar waters.

If you lose your faith, you will probably do so gradually. In tiny increments you will get spiritually sloppy. You will let a few days slip by without consulting your compass. Your sails will go untrimmed. Your rigging will go unprepared. And worst of all, you will forget to anchor your boat. And, before you know it, you'll be bouncing from wave to wave in stormy seas.

And unless you anchor deep, you could go down.

How do you anchor deep? Look at the verse again.

"We must pay more careful attention, therefore, to *what we have heard. . . .* "

Stability in the storm comes not from seeking a new message, but from understanding an old one. The most reliable anchor points are not recent discoveries, but are time-tested truths that have held their ground against the winds of change. Truths like:

My life is not futile.

My failures are not fatal.

My death is not final.

Attach your soul to these boulders and no wave is big enough to wash you under.

My prayer is that *Six Hours, One Friday* has been a tool to help you anchor to these rocks.

The following study guide will help you even more. It is ideal for personal devotional time, small group study or classroom exploration. The guide invites you to reexamine each chapter of the book on three levels.

Level One: Mind Anchors. This first part gleans crucial quotes from the chapter and invites you to reexamine them by answering some probing questions.

Level Two: Soul Anchors. This section uses parallel Scriptures to reinforce and clarify the thrust of the chapter.

Level Three: Life Anchors. Here is where you take the message home. Want to keep from drifting? Spend some time meditating over the exercises in this section.

I am deeply indebted to Steve Halliday and Liz Heaney for their work on this study guide.

One final word. Don't be content to depend on someone else's anchor points. Don't settle for a faith inherited from your family or borrowed from your friends. Their help is important and their teaching is vital, but you never know when you'll have to face a hurricane alone. So be sure that *your* heart is safely secured. Take the advice of the sailor, "Anchor deep, say a prayer and hold on!"

CHAPTER 1
HURRICANE WARNINGS

Mind Anchors

I.   *Anchor points. Firm rocks sunk deeply in a solid foundation. Not casual opinions or negotiable hypotheses, but ironclad undeniables that will keep you afloat. How strong are yours?*

1. Why are anchor points necessary in developing a strong life of faith? What happens if you don't have them?

2. What anchor points can you identify in your own life? How strong are they?

II.   *Three anchor points were planted firmly in bedrock two thousand years ago by a carpenter who claimed to be the Christ. And it was all done in the course of a single day. A single Friday. All done during six hours, one Friday.*

1. What does it mean that these anchor points were "planted firmly in bedrock"? What gives them such strength?

2. What set apart these six hours from any other six hours in history? Why is it remarkable that Jesus' work was accomplished in such a short time?

III.   *There is one stone to which you should tie. It's large. It's round. And it's heavy. It blocked the door of a grave. It wasn't big enough, though. The tomb it sealed was the tomb of a transient. He only went in to prove he could come out.*

1. In what sense was Jesus a "transient"? What Scripture verses can you think of that would say this in another way?

2. Why was it necessary for Jesus to "*prove* he could come out" of the tomb? Why leave evidence?

IV. *To the casual observer the six hours are mundane . . . but to the handful of awestruck witnesses the most maddening of miracles is occurring. God is on a cross. The creator of the universe is being executed. . . . And there is no one to save him, for he is sacrificing himself.*

1. How is the crucifixion of Jesus a "miracle"? What thoughts do you imagine went through Jesus' mind during his ordeal?

2. Why is it significant that Jesus sacrificed himself? How does your answer make you feel?

Soul Anchors

Read Hebrews 12:2-13

1. According to verses 2-3, what should Christians do to avoid growing weary or losing heart in the face of personal hurricanes? In what practical ways can this advice help you?

2. How do we sometimes "make light of" hardships or "lose heart" because of them? What use does God sometimes make of these hardships, according to verse 6?

3. What is an ultimate purpose of God in allowing "hurricanes" into our lives, according to verse 10?

4. How do we feel about these hardships, according to verse 11? Does it help to know that God understands how we feel about this? Why?

5. According to verse 11, what kind of people reap the benefits of such difficult experiences?

6. What connection is there between verse 12 and verses 2-3? What anchor points are mentioned in this passage?

Life Anchors

1. On a clean sheet of paper write down five of your personal anchor points. Put this list in a safe, accessible place and reread it when hurricanes blow into your life.

2. Think of the last time you went through a personal hurricane. How did you react? Did you rely on any anchor points? If not, why not? If so, which ones?

3. What do you think were Jesus' anchor points when he walked on this earth? Which ones do you think he relied upon while he spent those six hours on the cross?

4. Take five minutes to thank God for providing firm anchor points for your faith. If you haven't been relying on these anchor points as you should, confess it and ask the Lord to help you the next time a hurricane blows your way.

_____
CHAPTER 2
_____

GOD'S FORMULA FOR FATIGUE

Mind Anchors

I. *You are tired. You are weary. Weary of being slapped by the waves of broken dreams. Weary of being stepped on and run over in the endless marathon to the top. Weary of trusting in someone only to have that trust returned in an envelope with no return address.*

1. Have you ever felt this way? If so, explain. If not, think of someone you know who has felt this way. What caused such feelings?

II. Is it worth it? When I get what I want, will it be worth the price I paid? *Perhaps those were the thoughts of a San Antonio lawyer I read about recently. Apparently his success wasn't enough. One day, he came home, took a gun out of his vault, climbed into a sleeping bag, and took his life. His note to his bride read, "It's not that I don't love you. It's just that I'm tired and I want to rest."*

1. In what ways can weariness distort one's thinking?

2. Do you think this lawyer achieved what he was after? Why?

III. *Jesus was the only man to walk God's earth who claimed to have an answer for man's burdens. "Come to me," he invited them. My prayer is that you, too, will find rest. And that you will sleep like a baby.*

1. Many groups today claim to have an answer for man's problems. How is Jesus' answer different from theirs?

2. Describe this answer that Jesus claimed to have for man's burdens. How do you evaluate his answer?

3. Does this wish for "sleeping like a baby" mean that believers are shielded from situations that rob them of sleep? Explain.

Soul Anchors

Read Matthew 11:28-29

1. What kind of people does Jesus invite to come to him? What does he promise them?

2. The phrase "take my yoke upon you" is unfamiliar to many of us today. Read what William Hendriksen had to say about it and then answer the questions that follow:

> In Jewish literature a "yoke" represents the sum total of obligations which, according to *the teaching* of the rabbis, a person must take upon himself . . . . Because of their misinterpretation, alteration, and augmentation of God's holy law, the yoke which Israel's teachers placed upon the shoulders of the people was that of a totally unwarranted legalism. It was the system of *teaching* that stressed salvation by means of strict obedience to a host of rules and regulations. Now here in 11:29 Jesus places his own teaching over against that to which the people had become accustomed.

When he says, "Take my yoke upon you
and learn from me," . . . he means, "Accept my teaching, namely, that a person is
saved by means of simple trust in me. . . ."
Symbolically speaking, Jesus here assures
the oppressed persons whom he addresses,
both then and now, that *his* yoke, that is,
the one he urges them to wear, is kindly,
and his burden, that is, that which he re-
quires of us, is light. What he is really saying, therefore, is that simple trust in him
and obedience to his commands out of
gratitude for the salvation already im-
parted by him is delightful. It brings peace
and joy. The person who lives this kind of
life is no longer a slave. He has become
free.[1]

What "yokes" are you carrying today? How does
Jesus suggest you can shed them?

Read Hebrews 4:1-11

3. How does a person enjoy the rest of God?

4. How did some people in the past fail to enjoy
this rest?

5. What is the link between the rest mentioned
in Matthew 11:28-29 and that in Hebrews 4:1-11?

Life Anchors

1. Do you believe you normally enjoy the rest
Jesus provides? Why or why not? What things keep
you from enjoying it?

2. If it's your desire to enjoy Jesus' offer of rest,
but you're not sure what to do, begin with these
three things:

a. Reread chapter two, "God's Formula for Fatigue."

b. Read once more Matthew 11:28-29 and Hebrews 4:1-11.

c. Sit down with a piece of paper and a pencil and write out specific steps you find in these two sources which describe how to enjoy God's rest.

3. Keep a personal journal for one week, each day recording any events which keep you from enjoying the rest of Jesus. At the end of the week, do two things:

a. Pray about each of those events, asking God for his help in enjoying his rest. Be sure to thank him for those times when you did enjoy his rest.

b. Analyze the events, looking for clues which might indicate how you got off track.

1.William Hendricksen *The Gospel of Matthew* (Grand Rapids, Mich.: Baker Book House, 1973) pp. 504, 505.

<hr>

CHAPTER 3

TWO TOMBSTONES

Mind Anchors

I.   *"Sleeps, but rests not.*
Loved, but was loved not.
Tried to please, but pleased not.
Died as she lived—alone."

1. What for you is the most chilling phrase in this epitaph? Why?

2. If you were to write an epitaph for yourself that expresses your current lot in life, what would it say?

II.   *How many people will die in the loneliness in which they are living? The homeless in Atlanta. The happy-hour hopper in L.A. A bag lady in Miami. The preacher in Nashville. Any person who doubts whether the world needs him. Any person who is convinced that no one really cares.*

1. How do you identify people living in loneliness? What characterizes them outwardly?

2. What lonely people do you know?

3. Have you ever fit any of the descriptions in this passage? Which one(s)?

III.   *The woman asked the question that revealed the gaping hole in her soul. "Where is God? My people say he is on the mountain. Your people say he is in Jerusalem. I don't know where he is."*

1. Have you ever met someone who was asking these kinds of questions? What did you tell him or her?

2. Have you ever asked these questions yourself?
If so, what prompted the questions?

IV.   *Barbara's difficult home life had left her afraid
and insecure. While the other children talked,
she sat. While the others sang, she was silent.
While the others giggled, she was quiet. Always
present. Always listening. Always speechless.*

*Until the day Joy gave a class on heaven. Joy
talked about seeing God. She talked about tearless eyes and deathless lives. Barbara listened
with hunger. Then she raised her hand. "Mrs.
Joy?"*

"Yes, Barbara?"

"Is heaven for girls like me?"

1. Describe the emotional impact this story has
on you. Why is Barbara's question so poignant?

2. What do you think caused Barbara to ask such
a question?

3. If you had been Joy, how would you have
answered Barbara's question?

Soul Anchors

Read John 4:4-42

1. Jews of Jesus' day avoided passing through
Samaria at all costs, even taking long detours to
bypass the area. Yet John 4:4 says Jesus "had" to go
though Samaria. Why do you think he "had" to do
so?

2. How did Jesus use his own needs as tools for
evangelism (vv. 6-15)? What can we learn from this?

3. What is the "living water" Jesus talks about in verse 10? What does it do?

4. What kind of people does God seek to worship him (vv. 23-24)? Could this Samaritan woman qualify? Do you?

5. How did Jesus use his own needs as tools for teaching (vv. 31-38)? What can we learn from this?

6. How did the woman's report about Jesus affect the people of her town (vv. 39-42)? Taking into account her background (vv. 17-18), why is this remarkable?

7. Identify the single greatest lesson you have learned from this story.

Life Anchors

1. Sit down with a close friend or your spouse and write out what gives your life purpose and meaning. Be specific. The next time you are overwhelmed by the rising tides of futility, take out that list and read it.

2. Do you know any Grace Llewellen Smiths? What can you do to help make them feel more significant? Why not do it today?

CHAPTER 4

LIVING PROOF

Mind Anchors

I.   *One step into the classroom and the cat of curiosity pounced on Jenna. And I walked away. I gave my daughter up. Not much. And not as much as I will have to in the future. But I gave her up as much as I could today.*

1. In what other ways will Jenna (or your boy or girl) have to be given up in the future?

2. Does it help to know that all this "giving up" doesn't have to be done at once? Why?

II.   *I gave up my child fully aware that were she to need me I would be at her side in a heartbeat. You, God, said good-bye to your son fully aware that when he would need you the most, when his cry of despair would roar through the heavens, you would sit in silence. The angels, though positioned, would hear no command from you. Your son, though in anguish, would feel no comfort from your hands.*

1. Why did God give up his son so completely?

2. Imagine, if you can, what it might have been like in heaven's throneroom while Christ suffered on the cross. What is the mood of the angels surrounding God—somber? Sad? Happy? Angry? Confused?

III.   *Before the day was over, I sat in silence a second time. This time, not beside my daughter, but*

*before my Father. This time not sad over what I
had to give, but grateful for what I'd already
received—living proof that God does care.*

1. What is the "living proof" to which this passage refers?

2. How do you respond to this "living proof"?

Soul Anchors

Read Romans 8:32-39

1. For what purpose did God give up his son (v. 32)?

2. Finish the following phrase, based on the second half of verse 32: "Because God was willing to give up his only son for us, we should never think that he _____

_____

_____."

3. What does it mean that Christ even now "intercedes" for us (v. 34)? How does this make you feel?

4. In a passage of Scripture aimed at helping believers understand their safe position with God, what is Paul's point in quoting a text that says, "For your sake we face death all day long; we are considered as sheep to be slaughtered"?

5. What things, according to Paul, can separate a believer from the love of Christ (vv. 35-39)?

Life Anchors

1. Think about past hurricanes in your life. What gives you "living proof" that God loves you? Make a list of these specifics.

2. Do you help others experience your love for them? Who are the significant people in your life? Think of one thing you can give them as "living proof" of your love for them, and do it.

3. If you have not been able to experience God's love for you, ask God to open your heart so that you would recognize his hand in your life. Then go to a Christian friend whom you regard as spiritually mature and ask what he or she would do in your shoes.

CHAPTER 5

FLAMING TORCHES AND LIVING PROMISES

Mind Anchors

I. *Had any visits from Doubt lately? If you find yourself going to church in order to be saved and not because you are saved, then you've been listening to him. If you find yourself doubting if God could forgive you* again *for that, you've been sold some snake oil. If you are more cynical about Christians than sincere about Christ, then guess who came to dinner.*

1. Explain the phrase "If you find yourself going to church in order to be saved and not because you are saved, then you're listening to him." How is this statement a reflection of doubt?

2. To which lies of Doubt are you most susceptible?

II. *The invisible God had drawn near to Abraham to make his immovable promise: "To your descendants I give this land." And though God's people often forgot their God, God didn't forget them. He kept his word. The land became theirs. God didn't give up. He never gives up.*

1. In what situations are you most likely to forget God?

2. How does it make you feel to know that God "never gives up"? At what times in your life has this knowledge been especially comforting?

III. *So, the next time that obnoxious neighbor Doubt
     walks in, escort him out. Out to the hill. Out to
     Calvary. Out to the cross where, with holy blood,
     the hand that carried the flame wrote the prom-
     ise, "God would give up his only son before he'd
     give up on you."*

1. Why is Calvary a good place to put doubt to
rest?

Soul Anchors

Read 2 Timothy 2:8-13

1. One good way to combat doubt is to remember what things are essential. What does Paul ask
Timothy to "remember" in verse 8? How is this
essential?

2. Verse 11 promises that we will live with Christ
if we "died with him." What does it mean to "die
with him"? How do you do that?

3. How is "enduring" connected with
"reigning" in verse 12? How does this idea relate to
verse 10?

4. What warning is included in verse 12? How
does doubt sometimes enter in here? How does
Paul's warning here compare to Jesus' own words in
Luke 12:8-9?

5. What great hope is found in verse 13? Upon
what is this hope built?

6. What does it mean to you that God is absolutely faithful?

Life Anchors

1. This chapter has listed many times when God did not give up on his people. Think about your own life. Can you recall times when you were unfaithful, but God was faithful to you? Write these down and tell a friend about them.

2. Is doubt ever a good thing? Have there been times in your life when you looked your doubts in the face and they strengthened your faith? Talk about these times with a friend or write about them. How can this encourage you the next time doubt comes your way?

3. For more insight into doubt and God's faithfulness, read *Disappointment with God* by Philip Yancey.

CHAPTER 6

ANGELIC MESSAGES

Mind Anchors

I. *What if God had responded to my grumblings? What if he'd heeded my complaints? He could have. He could have answered my carelessly mumbled prayers. And had he chosen to do so, a prototype of the result had just appeared at my door.*

1. What prayers have *you* mumbled which you're glad God hasn't answered? Why do you think grumbling comes so easy to us?

2. What "angels" have crossed your path recently?

II. *God sent the boy with a message. And the point the boy made was razor-sharp: "You cry over spilled champagne. Your complaints are not over the lack of necessities but the abundance of benefits. You bellyache over the frills, not the basics; over benefits, not essentials. The source of your problems is your blessings."*

1. Do you believe God would make these same statements to you? Why or why not?

2. Try to name your personal "Top Ten Blessings."

III. *Gajowniczek survived the Holocaust. He made his way back to his hometown. Every year, however, he goes back to Auschwitz. Every August 14 he goes back to say thank you to the man who died in his place. In his back yard there is a plaque. On the plaque is a tribute he carved with his own hands. A tribute to Maximilian Kolbe—the man who died so Gajowniczek could live.*

1. What makes Gajowniczek trek back to Auschwitz every August 14? If you were in his place, would you continue the trips? Why?

2. The statement about Kolbe—"he died so that I could live"—is also a good way to think about Jesus' relationship to redeemed sinners. Explain how this is so.

Soul Anchors

Read John 11:45-52

1. In the verses just prior to this passage, John tells how Jesus had raised Lazarus from the dead. What happened because of this miracle (v. 45)? How did this make Lazarus an "angel" to others?

2. In what two ways did people respond to this "angel" (vv. 45-46; Luke 12:9-11)? In what ways can we respond to the "angels" God sends us?

3. What did *Caiaphas* mean by his speech in verses 49-50?

4. What did *God* mean by that same speech (vv. 51-52)?

5. How are these two interpretations of the same speech typical of the way God often works (see also Acts 4:24-28)?

6. For what purpose did Jesus die, according to verses 51-52? For whom did he die? Are you included in this list? If so, how?

Life Anchors

1. Who are the people for whom you are most grateful? Do they know how you feel? If not, tell them of your appreciation and why they mean so much to you. Ask God to help you encourage them in both the timing and the selection of your words.

2. Take a couple of hours this week to go with a friend and visit a homeless shelter or mission. Talk to the people there, finding out who they are and what has happened to them. Also talk with those who work there. What needs do their clients have? How does the community respond to the have-nots in your city? What might you do to help meet some of these needs?

CHAPTER 7

REMEMBER

Mind Anchors

I.   *The church of Jesus Christ began with a group of frightened men in a second-floor room in Jerusalem.*

1. What frightened these men?

2. Why do you think modern-day disciples are frightened?

II.   *The one betrayed sought his betrayers. What did he say to them? Not, "What a bunch of flops!" Not, "I told you so." No "Where-were-you-when-I-needed-you?" speeches. But simply one phrase, "Peace be with you." The very thing they didn't have was the very thing he offered: peace.*

1. How important is it that Jesus "sought his betrayers"? What likely would have happened if he hadn't done so?

2. What was the purpose behind Jesus' speech? Why did these men need it?

III.   *What unlocked the doors of the apostles' hearts? Simple. They saw Jesus. They encountered the Christ. Their sins collided with their Savior and their Savior won! What lit the boiler of the apostles was a red-hot conviction that the very one who should have sent them to hell went to hell for them and came back to tell about it.*

1. Explain the phrase "Their sins collided with their Savior and their Savior won!"

2. What should it matter to us how Jesus interacted with a group of men two thousand years ago?

IV. *Think about the first time you ever saw him. Think about your first encounter with the Christ. Robe yourself in that moment. Resurrect the relief. Recall the purity. Summon forth the passion. Can you remember?*

1. Describe the first time you "saw" Christ.

2. How long ago did you first "see Christ"? If you could climb in a time machine and revisit that moment, would you? Why?

V. *There is a direct correlation between the accuracy of our memory and the effectiveness of our mission. If we are not teaching people how to be saved, it is perhaps because we have forgotten the tragedy of being lost! If we're not teaching the message of forgiveness, it may be because we don't remember what it was like to be guilty. And if we're not preaching the cross, it could be that we've subconsciously decided that—God forbid—somehow we don't need it.*

1. Try to recall what it was like to be "lost." Describe it. Did you feel guilt? In what way(s)?

2. Do you think you need the cross? Why?

VI. *A man is never the same after he simultaneously sees his utter despair and Christ's unbending grace. To see the despair without the grace is suicidal. To see the grace without the despair is upper room futility. But to see them both is conversion.*

1. Why are both "despair" and "grace" necessary for conversion?

Soul Anchors

Read Acts 23:6-15

1. For what reason was Paul in custody at this time (v. 6)? Would there have been an uproar had he kept silent about Jesus? Explain.

2. What incident gave Paul great strength and courage in the midst of his hardships (v. 11)? How would this have helped?

3. Did the Lord's promise of help shield Paul from trouble (vv. 12-15)? What did the promise secure for Paul?

4. What is it about seeing Jesus that gives boldness and strength?

5. Can you "see Jesus" without having an actual vision of him? If so, how?

Life Anchors

1. Take about half an hour and meditate on the cross. You could do this in several ways—

    a. Remember who you are and who Jesus is and what he did for you. What is it about Jesus that particularly amazes you?

    b. Use a familiar hymnbook and focus on hymns about the cross. Try reading them aloud or singing them.

    c. Ask God to fill you with awe that
       he—the God of the universe—
       would die for you. Read Psalm 22
       and use it to guide your thoughts.

2. Find a partner and take turns asking the following questions. Write down your answers, but don't evaluate what was said until all questions are answered. Say what you really think, not what you believe you should think.

    a. What does Jesus think about your
       relationship with him? How would
       he describe it?

    b. How does he view you?

    c. How do you view him?

    d. Do you believe he would offer you
       peace as he did the disciples, or do
       you think he would reprimand
       you? Why?

Once the questions have been answered, go over them together and summarize what your answers reveal.

3. What hardships are you facing right now? Write these down and beside each note how Jesus can help you weather this storm.

CHAPTER 8

FATAL ERRORS

Mind Anchors

I. *Could you do it all over again, you'd do it differently. You'd be a different person. You'd be more patient. You'd control your tongue. You'd finish what you started. You'd turn the other cheek instead of slapping his. You'd get married first. You wouldn't marry at all. You'd be honest. You'd resist the temptation. You'd run with a different crowd.*

But you can't. And as many times as you tell yourself, "What's done is done," what you did can't be undone.

1. What major decisions or actions in your own life would you change if you could?

2. What dangers are there in rehearsing past personal errors? What benefits?

II. *Don't we all long for a father who, even though our mistakes are written all over the wall, will love us anyway? Don't we want a father who cares for us in spite of our failures?*

1. How would you answer these questions? Why would you answer like this?

III. *What kind of heavenly father do we have? A father who is at his best when we are at our worst. A father whose grace is strongest when our devotion is weakest.*

1. What specific comfort do you receive from

the thought in this passage? What does this statement mean for you?

2. Name three instances where you experienced the truth of this passage.

Soul Anchors

Compare Acts 13:13 and 15:36-41 to 2 Timothy 4:11

1. Describe the failure of John Mark. How serious, in Paul's mind, was this failure?

2. What happened in Acts 15:36-41 as a direct result of this failure?

3. The text doesn't mention how John Mark felt about this controversy. If you were in his shoes, what might you have felt?

4. How does 2 Timothy 4:11 show that Mark's failure was not fatal? What had changed over time?

5. What lessons can you learn from the experience of John Mark?

Life Anchors

1. If you find it difficult to believe that God accepts your failures, begin with these two things:

    a. Reread "Fatal Errors," slowly and meditatively, asking God to let the truths of the chapter sink into your soul.

    b. Go back to the story of John Mark in Acts 13:13 and 15:36-41, then write out the lesson you learn from

John Mark and how you can apply
this lesson to your life.

2. If you have trouble experiencing God's grace,
it will take time for you to feel free of your guilt. Over
the next week, take time to identify those things
which keep you from accepting failure as a normal
part of life. Here are some things to think through
and write down:

> a. Do you have specific memories of
>   times when you have failed and
>   then been punished?
>
> b. How have the significant people in
>   your life affected your view of
>   failure?
>
> c. Can you remember times when
>   you have failed and the results
>   were used for good in your life?

3. Analyze how you responded to the questions
above and then pray that God will renew your mind
and help you see yourself as he sees you.

CHAPTER 9
CRISTO REDENTOR

Mind Anchors

I.   What kind of redeemer is this? *I thought.*
Blind eyes and stony heart? *I've since learned
the answer to my own question: exactly the kind
of redeemer most people have.*

1. Do you agree with this observation? Explain
your answer.

2. What kind of redeemer do you think your
next-door neighbor has? Your closest co-worker?
You?

II.   *In her despair the woman looks at the Teacher.
His eyes don't glare. "Don't worry," they whisper, "it's okay." And for the first time that morning she sees kindness.*

1. Imagine that you are this woman. What would
you have *expected* to see in Jesus' eyes? What is running through your mind?

2. Does this passage mean that Jesus winks at
sin? What does it mean?

III.   *On earth, Jesus was an artist in a gallery of his
own paintings. He was a composer listening as
the orchestra interpreted his music. He was a
poet hearing his own poetry. Yet his works of art
had been defaced, creation after battered creation. He had created people for splendor. They
had settled for mediocrity. He had formed them
with love. They had scarred each other with hate.*

1. How are these images of "artist," "composer," and "poet" meant to remind us of Jesus? To what aspects of his personality or work do they refer?

2. Give five specific, personally-observed examples that illustrate the point of this passage.

IV.   *"Is there no one to condemn you?" Jesus asked. There is still one who can, she thinks. And she turns to look at him.* What does he want? What will he do?

1. Why does the woman think, "There is still one who can"?

2. What do you think Jesus wants of *you?*

V.   *She would recognize his eyes. How could she ever forget those eyes? Clear and tear-filled. Eyes that saw her not as she was, but as she was intended to be.*

1. What did Jesus intend this woman to be? What does he intend you to be?

2. Does this passage give you hope? Why?

Soul Anchors

Read Luke 7:36-50

1. What things does the woman in this story have in common with the woman described in John 8?

2. What do you see in the eyes of this Pharisee when he looks at the woman (see verse 39)?

3. Compare the way Jesus dealt with the woman in this passage to the way he interacted with the

woman of John 8. What things did he do similarly? What did he do differently?

4. What is the point of the story Jesus tells in verses 41-43? With which character in the story do you most identify? Why?

5. How would you answer the question raised in verse 49?

6. Do you think Jesus could repeat his words found in verse 50 to you? Why or why not?

Life Anchors

1. Ask your closest friend to tell you honestly what your behavior reveals about the kind of redeemer you have. Find out *why* he or she says this and make any changes you see are necessary.

2. Reread the story in Luke 7:41-43. Write down the sins for which you have been forgiven—be sure to mention only those for which you have *experienced* God's forgiveness.

3. If you do not feel as if God has forgiven you for much, pray that he will make you sensitive to the sin in your life. If you feel that your sins are so terrible that a holy God could not forgive you, read this chapter again, putting yourself in the place of the woman.

CHAPTER 10

THE GOLDEN GOBLET

Mind Anchors

I.   *"The choice is hers," the King instructed. "If she turns to us for help, that is your command to deliver her. If she doesn't turn, if she doesn't look to me—don't go. The choice is hers."*

1. With help so near, why do you think the woman chose as she did?

2. Why do you think God refused to send help unless the woman asked for it?

II.   *"Their choice will be honored. Where there is poison, there will be death. Where there are goblets, there will be fire. Let it be done."*

1. In your own words, describe the spiritual principle outlined in this passage.

III.   *"I will taste the poison," swore the King's Son. "For this I have come. But the hour will be mine to choose."*

1. What did the son mean by, "I will taste the poison"? How was his "tasting" different from all those who had tasted before?

2. What was important about the son choosing the hour of his "tasting"? What is significant about the timing?

IV.   *"Here is the cup, my Son. Drink it alone."*

God must have wept as he performed his task. Every lie, every lure, every act done in shadows

*was in that cup. Slowly, hideously they were
absorbed into the body of the Son. The final act of
incarnation. The Spotless Lamb was blemished.
Flames began to lick his feet . . . . The King turns
away from his Prince. The undiluted wrath of a
sin-hating Father falls upon his sin-filled Son.
The fire envelops him. The shadow hides him.
The Son looks for his Father, but his Father
cannot be seen.*

"My God, my God . . . why?"

1. What one word would you pick to describe
how the son must have felt at the moment he drank
the cup?

2. Do you think an answer to the son's agonized
question would have eased his pain? Explain your
answer.

V.   *A noise snaps the King from his dream. He
opens his eyes and sees a transcendent figure
gleaming in the doorway. "It is finished, Father.
I have come home."*

1. What emotional impact do these lines have
upon you?

2. What part of this story is most memorable for
you? Why?

Soul Anchors

Read 2 Corinthians 5:21

1. Who "had no sin"? What does this mean?

2. How did this one "become sin" for us? What was the purpose?

Read Galatians 3:13-14

3. How did Christ "redeem us from the curse of the law"? When did this happen?

4. What was the purpose for Christ's becoming a curse for us?

5. How do we receive "the promise of the Spirit"?

Read Romans 8:3-4

6. Why was the law "powerless" to bring us to God?

7. How did God overcome this powerlessness?

8. If sinful men are unable to meet the requirements of the law, how can they be saved (v. 4)?

Life Anchors

1. "The Golden Goblet" paints a picture of the spiritual warfare that raged in Eden, but that warfare continues all around us. Are you currently engaged in a spiritual struggle? What is it? Describe it to a friend and ask for prayer that you will embrace God's help to win the battle. Ask to be held accountable.

2. Pray that God will make you more sensitive to spiritual warfare and the power of prayer to defeat Satan.

3. For more insight into spiritual warfare, read *Counterattack* by Jay Carty or *This Present Darkness* by Frank Peretti.

_____CHAPTER 11_____

COME HOME

Mind Anchors

I.   *Pride is made of stone. Hard knocks may chip it,*
but it takes reality's sledgehammer to break it.

    1. In what sense is pride "made of stone"?

    2. Why is it hard for the proud to accept the gospel?

II.   *His first few days of destitution were likely*
steamy with resentment. He was mad at every-
one. Everyone was to blame. His friends
shouldn't have bailed out on him. And his
brother should come and bail him out. His boss
should feed him better and his dad never should
have let him go in the first place.

    He named a pig after each one of them.

    1. Is it easy for you to blame others for your own mistakes? Explain.

    2. What gave the young man satisfaction in naming a pig after each one of the people mentioned? Do you ever act like this? How?

III. *It is so familiar: Cries for help muffled behind*
costumed faces. Fear hidden behind a painted
smile. Signals of desperation thought to be signs
of joy. Tell me that doesn't describe our world.

    1. In what ways does this describe your world?

    2. In what ways does this describe you?

IV. *He was going home a changed man. Not demanding that he get what he deserved, but willing to take whatever he could get. "Give me" had
been replaced with "help me," and his defiance
had been replaced with repentance.*

1. What factors helped cause this man's transformation?

2. Try to think of someone you know who has gone through a similar transformation. Describe them before/after.

V. *Jesus stretched his hands as open as he could. He
forced his arms so wide apart that it hurt. And to
prove that those arms would never fold and those
hands would never close, he had them nailed
open.*

They still are.

1. What does the last phrase mean?

2. What significance does this passage have for you?

Soul Anchors

Read Luke 15:11-32

1. What drove this young man to reconsider his way of living (vv. 14-16)? How is this story often replayed in the modern world?

2. Compare what the young man says in verse 18 to what King David said in Psalm 51:4. What sentiment is the same in both?

3. How does the father in verse 20 picture our heavenly father? Do you think it is a good picture? Why?

4. Compare verses 18-19 with verse 21. Note which part of the son's prepared speech gets left off. Why do you think the son was unable to finish the whole prepared speech?

5. Was the young man worthy of the treatment he received in verses 22-24? How is this scene a picture of grace?

6. Have you ever felt like the older brother in verses 25-30? Explain.

7. How is the father's description of his son in verse 32 a good description of every Christian?

Life Anchors

1. For the next week or so, carefully monitor what you do when you catch yourself making a mistake. Do you own up to your faults? Are you critical of yourself or do you tend to blame others? What sort of things do you say to yourself? Write down your observations and use them to guide your prayer schedule.

2. Ask someone you trust to name which of the three characters in Luke 15:1-32 you most resemble. Have your friend describe what he or she sees in you that prompts that response. With this input, consider whether you need to make some changes in your behavior and attitude. Choose three things you can do to help make those changes.

3. Take some time this week to think about how you believe God views your failures. Here are some questions to ask yourself:

    a. Do I have any failures from which I have never recovered?

    b. If I were to die and go to heaven today, what would Jesus say to me about my life?

    c. Can I see positive outcomes from my failures?

4. For more insight into how you can change, read *Inside Out* by Larry Crabb.

CHAPTER 12

THE FISH AND THE FALLS

Mind Anchors

I.   *The fish swam to where the water crashed into the river. He attempted to swim upwards. He would ascend the falls by brute force. But the onrush of the water was too strong. Undaunted, he swam until he could swim no more, then he slept.*

1. How does this passage picture man's attempt to reach God by unaided human strength? What is the outcome?

II.   *But how do you not hear the yearning of your heart? How do you turn away from discovery? How can you be satisfied with existence once you've lived with purpose?*

1. How would you answer these questions?
2. What purpose is there in your life?

III.   *All of nature watched as the fish rode the wave of grace. All of nature rejoiced when he reached the top. The stars raced through the blackness. The moon tilted backwards and rocked in sweet satisfaction. Bears danced. Birds hugged. The wind whistled. And the leaves applauded. The fish was where he had longed to be. He was in the presence of the roar.*

What he couldn't do the river had done. He knew immediately he would spend forever relishing the mystery.

1. How is the scene depicted here like Jesus' own statement in Luke 15:10?

2. How is the wave like God's grace? In what way is the fish like you? Where would the fish be without the wave? Where would you be without God's grace?

Soul Anchors

Read Romans 5:6-11

1. What word does Paul use to describe our inability to save ourselves (v. 6)? Why is this tough to swallow?

2. For whom did Christ die (v. 6)? Who could be characterized like this?

3. How does Paul try to get us to see the enormity of God's sacrifice for us in verses 7-8?

4. By what are Christians "justified" (v. 9)? How does this relate to the cross?

5. From what will all Christians be saved (v. 9)? What makes this possible?

6. How does Paul teach that people can go from being God's "enemies" in verse 10 to "rejoicing in God" in verse 11? What does it mean to "rejoice in God"?

Life Anchors

1. Do you know anyone who is struggling to understand the concept of God's grace? Do you know someone who has trouble believing that God's acceptance and approval have nothing to do with

our efforts? Who is that person? What can you do to help be a picture of grace to him or her?

2. Think through the gospel message as clearly as you can, making sure you identify all the major parts (see especially 1 Corinthians 15:1-11; Ephesians 2:8-9). Then "borrow" a child (not your own) from a close friend or neighbor and see if you can successfully communicate this message to him or her. Do a "debriefing" session afterwards where you evaluate how you did.

CHAPTER 13

THE ELEVENTH HOUR GIFT

Mind Anchors

I.   *And now, one more beggar comes with a request. Only minutes from the death of them both, he stands before the King. He will ask for crumbs. And he, like the others, will receive a whole loaf.*

1. What are the "crumbs" this man asked for? What was the "whole loaf" he received?

2. Why did the beggar receive such a great gift? How is this a picture of grace?

II.   *It's an inexplicable dilemma—how two people can hear the same words and see the same Savior, and one see hope and the other see nothing but himself.*

1. Describe a contemporary example of what this passage teaches.

III.   *Lodged in the thief's statement are the two facts that anyone needs to recognize in order to come to Jesus. Look at the phrase again. Do you see them?*

"We are getting what we deserve. This man has done nothing wrong."

1. Name the two facts that must be recognized in order for someone to come to Jesus.

2. What makes these two facts indispensable for coming to Jesus?

Soul Anchors

Read Colossians 1:21-23

1. Before the Colossians became Christians, what was their relationship to God (v. 21)? What areas of their lives were affected?

2. Who made the first move toward reconciliation (v. 22)?

3. How did God accomplish this reconciliation? What was his purpose in doing so (v. 22)?

4. How does one gain this new relationship to God (v. 23)?

5. Paul says the gospel holds great "hope." What hope in the gospel is there for you?

6. What does Paul mean when he says that he has become a servant of the gospel? How can we follow his example?

Life Anchors

1. Who are the people God has placed in your life? Consider neighbors, friends, co-workers, relatives, and service people. What message of God's grace do they hear from you? Why not decide today to make a conscious effort to tell one of these people the hope of the gospel? Plan out how and when you will do this.

2. Think about someone in your life who has treated you poorly or unfairly. Now suppose this person has come to you to ask your forgiveness. What will you do? In order to answer honestly, ask yourself these questions—

a. Am I a forgiving person—or do I hold grudges?

b. Can I remember specific incidents when a person asked for my forgiveness? What was my response?

c. Have I ever been refused forgiveness? If so, how might this affect my ability to forgive someone else?

CHAPTER 14

GOD VS. DEATH

Mind Anchors

I. *At that moment I stopped looking at the names
    and stared at the monument. I relaxed my focus
    from the lettering and looked at the tablet. What
    I saw was sobering. I saw myself. I saw my own
    reflection. My face looked at me from the shiny
    marble. It reminded me that I, too, have been
    dying as long as I have been living. I, too, will
    someday have my named carved in a granite
    stone. Someday I, too, will face death.*

1. What circumstances or events prompt you to ponder your own death?

2. What feelings do thoughts of your own death create in you? Why?

II. *Jesus unmasked death and exposed him for who
     he really is—a ninety-eight-pound weakling
     dressed up in a Charles Atlas suit. Jesus had no
     patience for this impostor. He couldn't sit still
     while death pulled the veil over life.*

1. In what way is death an "impostor"? How is it "a ninety-eight-pound weakling dressed up in a Charles Atlas suit"?

2. Why couldn't Jesus "sit still while death pulled the veil over life"?

III. *If you ever want to know how to conduct yourself
      at a funeral, don't look to Jesus for an example.
      He interrupted each one he ever attended.*

1. How might this statement make you smile?

2. What point was Jesus making by interrupting all these funerals? How was this important?

Soul Anchors

Read Hebrews 2:14-16

1. What two reasons are given in verses 14-15 for Christ becoming human and dying on the cross?

2. How is it ironic that Christ's death was God's means of destroying the devil?

3. How does death hold people in slavery? Does it hold you? Why or why not?

4. Who is included in "Abraham's descendants" (see also Romans 4:16-17; Galatians 3:26-29)?

5. What advantage do redeemed men and women have over angels (v. 16)?

Life Anchors

1. One of the most exciting results of the gospel is that the Christian does not have to fear death. Death *is* an impostor. Take some time this week to delight in this truth. Look up 1 Corinthians 15:51-57. Meditate on these verses, asking God to let the wonder of his power over death encourage you.

2. If, after reading this chapter, you realize you have some fears about your own dying, try some of these ideas to help fortify your faith.

    a. Talk to someone about your fears. Ask for help in sorting out the rational from the irrational. Make a list of those fears which you need to overcome.

b. Find out the name of someone who has faced death and has experienced God's peace. Ask the person how he or she feels and why. What can you learn from this person that would help you?

CHAPTER 15

FANTASY OR REALITY?

Mind Anchors

I. *The followers of Jesus stop and step aside as the funeral procession shadows by. The blanket of mourning muffles the laughter of the disciples. No one spoke. What could they say? They feel the same despair felt by the bystanders at any funeral. "Someday that will be me." No one intervened. What could they do? Their only choice was to stand and stare as the mourners shuffled past.*

1. Think of the last funeral you attended. What parts of this description fit what you saw there?

2. Does it bother you to ponder your own mortality? Why?

II. *How would you feel at a moment like this? What would you do? A stranger tells you not to weep as you look at your dead son. One who refuses to mourn in the midst of sorrow calls the devil's bluff, then shocks you with a call into the cavern of death. Suddenly what had been taken is returned. What had been stolen is retrieved. What you had given up, you are given back.*

1. Answer the questions in the first two sentences of the passage.

2. How do you picture Jesus' demeanor in this incident? How do you picture that of the disciples?

III.   *Jesus gave the woman much more than her son.*
       He gave her a secret—a whisper that was over-
       heard by us. "That," he said pointing at the cot,
       "that is fantasy. This," he grinned, putting an
       arm around the boy, "this is reality."

1. In your own words, describe the secret Jesus whispered to the woman.

Soul Anchors

Read Luke 7:11-17

1. How did the Lord react when he saw this distraught mother (v. 13)? How is this typical of him?

2. Did the Lord require the mother to exercise faith before he performed the miracle?

3. The text doesn't tell us, but what do you imagine the young man might have said after Jesus raised him from the dead (v. 15)?

4. How did the people respond to Jesus' miracle?

5. Did the people fully understand who Jesus was? How can you tell?

6. Why is it that believers today do not seem as intent on "spreading the news" about Jesus as were the people back then (v. 17)?

Life Anchors

1. Do you know someone who is dying or who has recently lost a person he or she cared about?

What can you do to encourage him or her? Here are some suggestions—

> a. Read him the last section of this book.
>
> b. Spend time with her and listen to any of her fears.
>
> c. Pray with him about those fears.
>
> d. Commit yourself to pray for her and to keep in contact so she doesn't feel abandoned.

2. Make a list of some practical things you could do to help someone who was dying. Some things to include are:

> a. Help with meals and transportation.
>
> b. Help with correspondence and communication.
>
> c. Volunteer to take care of the children.
>
> d. Offer to help make sure his or her financial affairs are in order, or identify someone who can.

Keep this list in a place of easy access so that when the time comes you are ready to help.

3. If you have never lost a loved one, you may feel uncomfortable around those who are grieving. A classic on the subject is *The Last Thing We Talk About* by Joe Bayley.

<hr>

CHAPTER 16

THE SPARKLE FROM ETERNITY

Mind Anchors

I.   *Wallace had never known such helplessness. He didn't know how to handle his pain. He was so accustomed to being strong, he didn't know how to be weak. He assured all who called that his daughter was fine. He assured all who inquired that God was a great God. He assured everyone but himself.*

1. Why do you think it is hard for "strong" people to show weakness? How is this sometimes a handicap?

2. Do you ever feel that God is not as great as you say he is? Explain.

II.   *Wallace began to weigh his options. Should he go to see the Teacher? "If I go and am recognized, it will mean my job. But if she dies and he could have done something. . . ." A man reaches a point where his desperation is a notch above his dignity. He shrugs his shoulders. "What choice do I have?"*

1. Have you ever reached a point of desperation similar to Wallace's? What happened?

2. What is it about trying circumstances that often brings people to Jesus?

III. *This Jesus looked too normal. He wore a corduroy jacket, the kind with patches on the elbows.*

His slacks weren't new, but they were nice. No tie. His hairline receded a bit before it became a flow of brown curls. I couldn't hear his voice, but I could see his face. His eyebrows were bushy. He had a gleam in his eyes and a grin on his lips— as if he were watching you unwrap the birthday present he just gave you.

1. If Jesus were to appear on earth today, do you think this description might fit him? Why or why not?

2. How do you normally picture Jesus?

IV. *Wallace regretted the words as soon as he said them.* If he's a man, then I've asked the impossible. If he's more than a man, what right do I have to make such a request?

1. Where do you agree or disagree with Wallace's reasoning?

2. What would the granting of Wallace's request imply about the identity of Jesus?

V. *Peace where there should be pain. Confidence in the midst of crisis. Hope defying despair. That's what that look says. It is a look that knows the answer to the question asked by every mortal: "Does death have the last word?" I can see Jesus wink as he gives the answer. "Not on your life."*

1. Are you confident that Jesus has mastered death? Why or why not?

2. How does your answer to the previous question affect the way you live?

Soul Anchors

Read Mark 5:21-43

1. Why were large crowds always following Jesus? Had you been alive at the time, do you believe you would have been among them? Why?

2. What was important to Jesus about identifying the woman who had been healed of her affliction? Why not just overlook it?

3. What does Jesus' declaration to the woman (v. 34) have in common with his instruction to Jairus (v. 36)?

4. What reasons can you name to explain why Jesus required Jairus to show faith, but not the distraught mother of Luke 7:11-17? What might this suggest about the way God works in the world?

5. Note how Jesus gave orders for the little girl to be fed after he raised her from the dead (v. 43). What does this tell you about Jesus?

Life Anchors

1. Did you notice how Jesus responded to Jairus's request for help? Even though he was busy, Jesus didn't hesitate: "Jesus went with him" (Mark 5:24).

How receptive are you to cries for help? Do your friends see you as a caring and compassionate person—someone they can call on if they are in need? Whom do you feel free to call on? Ask those people if they feel the same toward you, and why.

2. Look more closely at those people you cited as being willing to help. What qualities or characteristics do they have that make them approachable? Write these down and evaluate your own strengths in these areas. If you see that you need to change, you can begin the process by—

    a. Praying that God will help you grow in those areas in which you are weak.

    b. Choosing one or two characteristics that you can begin to cultivate today. Decide how you can do that.

    c. Ask someone to give you feedback on any changes he or she sees in you.

3. Why wait until someone asks you for help? What could you do today that would help or encourage someone? Go do it.

CHAPTER 17
ROUND THREE: "LAZARUS, COME OUT!"

Mind Anchors

I.   *A life wasted pacing up and down in a self-made cell of fear. It is shocking. It is tragic. It is a pity. And it is also very common.*

1. Give several examples of what this passage describes.

2. Have you ever wasted part of your life "pacing up and down in a self-made cell of fear"? How did you escape?

II.   *Jesus wept. He wept not for the dead but for the living. He wept not for the one in the cave of death but for those in the cave of fear. He wept for those who, though alive, were dead. He wept for those who, though free, were prisoners, held captive by their fear of death.*

1. How can someone be "alive" yet "dead"?

2. What does Jesus' weeping tell you about his character or personality? How does this affect your perception of him?

III.   *Jesus saw people enslaved by their fear of a cheap power. He explained that the river of death was nothing to fear. The people wouldn't believe him. He touched a boy and called him back to life. The followers were still unconvinced. He whispered life into the dead body of a girl. The people were still cynical. He let a dead man spend four days in a grave and then called him out. Is*

*that enough? Apparently not. For it was neces-
sary for him to enter the river, to submerge himself in the water of death before people would
believe that death had been conquered.*

1. How was Jesus' resurrection different from
the boy's, the girl's, or Lazarus's?

2. Do you believe that Jesus has conquered
death? Why or why not?

Soul Anchors

Read John 11:1-44

1. How could Jesus say in verse 4, "This sickness
will not *end* in death," when he knew very well that
Lazarus would die?

2. How was Jesus glorified through this incident,
as he predicted in verse 4?

3. In what way are verses 25-26 the heart of the
gospel? How do you respond to Jesus' question here?

4. What was Jesus doing that caused the Jews to
say of his relationship to Lazarus, "See how he loved
him!" (v. 36)? How do his actions color your picture
of him?

5. Compare Martha's words in verse 27 to those
in verse 39. Does her faith remind you of your own at
times? If so, how?

6. What is the strongest impression you get of
Jesus from reading these three stories of his resur-
recting the dead?

Life Anchors

1. Make an appointment to visit a funeral home. Ask the funeral director questions about his arranging of funeral details, how he deals with those in grief, the differences between "religious" and "secular" services, his personal view of death, etc. When you return home, write a page or two describing how your visit affected your views of death and Christianity.

2. The next time you see a movie or television show which includes scenes of death, ask yourself how the show's producers picture death. Do they see it as final? Triumphant? Glorious? Frightening? Then sit down with a family member or friend and try to imagine how you, as a director with a Christian viewpoint, would have staged those same scenes. What would you do differently? The same?

CHAPTER 18

THE CELEBRATION

Mind Anchors

I.   *"Why are you crying?" An uncommon question
     to be asked in a cemetery. In fact, the question is
     rude. That is, unless the questioner knows some-
     thing the questionee doesn't.*

1. What did the questioner know that the questionee didn't?

2. Of what significance is this knowledge?

II. *Jesus doesn't leave her wondering long, just long
     enough to remind us that he loves to surprise us.
     He waits for us to despair of human strength
     and then intervenes with heavenly. God waits
     for us to give up and then—surprise!*

1. Why do you think Jesus "waits for us to despair of human strength"?

2. Have you experienced any of God's surprises?
Describe them.

III. *"Miriam," Jesus said softly, "surprise!"*

     *Mary was shocked. It's not often you hear your
     name spoken by an eternal tongue. But when she
     did, she recognized it. And when she did, she
     responded correctly. She worshiped him.*

1. Why was worship Mary's correct response?
What does it mean to worship?

2. What is the correct response to Jesus today?
How are you responding to him?

Soul Anchors

Read John 20:1-18

1. What was Mary's concern when she saw the stone rolled away from Jesus' tomb?

2. What was remarkable about the items Peter and John found in the tomb (vv. 5-7)? What made John "believe" (v. 8)?

3. Three times Mary expresses her belief that someone has carried away the dead body of Jesus (vv. 2, 13, 15). What makes her change her belief (v. 16)?

4. What task did Jesus give Mary to do? What did she do?

5. Are you glad that God is a God of surprises? Explain your answer.

Life Anchors

1. Since God invites us to share in his work, and since he is a God of surprises, plan and give a surprise party or event for a friend who wouldn't expect it.

2. Keep a personal journal for two weeks in which you record any surprises God springs on you during that time. At the end of the two weeks, take your journal and go someplace quiet where you can thank him for these special works in your life. Pray also that you might respond well to any surprises that aren't so welcome.

3. Celebrate the resurrection with your family or friends. Some ideas include:

a. Have communion and a time of worship.

b. Present a gift to someone who cannot return the favor.

c. Attend a theatrical performance or rent a movie that highlights Jesus' victory over death.

d. Identify an unbelieving friend and ask that person to read and give his or her reaction to one of the chapters in this section of the book.

e. Discuss as a group how your lives would be different if the resurrection had never happened.

CHAPTER 19

THE FINAL GLANCE

Mind Anchors

I. *My dad left me with a final look. One last statement of the eyes. One farewell message from the captain before the boat would turn out to sea. One concluding assurance from a father to a son, "It's all right."*

1. The phrase "it's all right" pops up frequently in this book, even in this story of a dying father. What's the point?

2. For whom does the phrase "it's all right" fit? For whom does it not fit?

II. *For a long while the centurion sat on a rock and stared at the three silhouetted figures. Their heads were limp, occasionally rolling from side to side. The jeering was silent, eerily silent. . . . Suddenly the center head ceased to bob. It yanked itself erect. Its eyes opened in a flash of white. A roar silenced the silence. "It is finished." It wasn't a yell. It wasn't a scream. It was a roar, a lion's roar. From what world that roar came the centurion didn't know, but he knew it wasn't this one.*

1. What was "finished" in this story? Why was it said so forcefully?

2. Many Christians find great hope and comfort in these three words, "It is finished." Why?

III.   *Had the centurion not said it, the soldiers would*
       have. Had the centurion not said it, the rocks
       would have—as would have the angels, the
       stars, even the demons. But he did say it. It fell to
       a nameless foreigner to state what they all knew.
       "Surely this man was the Son of God."

   1. If the centurion fully understood his words, what course of action should he have taken?

   2. If it is true that Jesus is the Son of God, what course of action should you take? What is your relationship to him?

Soul Anchors

Read Mark 15:33-39

   1. What statement was God making by causing darkness to fall over the land for three solid hours during the height of the afternoon?

   2. Read through Psalm 22:1-18. This portion of Scripture was written hundreds of years before Christ was born, yet it contains detailed descriptions of what would happen at the crucifixion. What details presented in Psalm 22 can you match with the gospel account in Mark 15?

   3. What prompted the centurion to say of Jesus, "Surely this man was the Son of God!" (v. 39)?

   4. Who do you think Jesus is? On what basis do you give your answer?

Life Anchors

   1. Pick a favorite spot where you can be alone and think. Go there and spend some time reflecting

on how this book has challenged you to change certain aspects of your life. What specific changes is God asking you to make in:

Your family life?

Your work life?

Your church life?

Your relationship to friends?

Your reading habits?

Your recreational time?

Your spending priorities?

Your giving patterns?

Your use of time?

Your conversation or vocabulary?

Other areas?

2. Write a letter to a close friend, expressing how this book has changed your view of God. Be as personal and specific as possible.

Max Lucado preaches weekly at the Oak Hills Church of Christ in San Antonio, Texas. If you would like to order tapes of his messages, you can request a tape catalog from:

Upwords Tape Ministry
8308 Fredricksburg Road
San Antonio, Texas 78229